THE
FORSYTE
SAGA

THE OFFICIAL COMPANION

Rupert Smith was a lecturer in theatre history before he fell into journalism, writing on all aspects of arts and entertainment from Diana Ross to Mahler, from *EastEnders* to *The Forsyte Saga*. He writes regularly for the *Guardian* and *Radio Times* and is the author of three novels and two biographies.

THE
FORSYTE
SAGA

THE OFFICIAL COMPANION

RUPERT SMITH

GRANADA

The Forsyte Saga is a Granada Media Production for ITV1

First published in Great Britain in 2002
By Granada Media, an imprint of André Deutsch Limited, part of the Carlton Publishing Group.
20 Mortimer Street
London W1T 3JW

In association with Granada Media Group
Text copyright © Granada Media Group Ltd 2002

A catalogue record for this book is available from the British Library.

Chapter 1 photographs courtesy of:

Pg10/11 Karl Marx, Mary Evans Picture Library; King Edward VIII, Mary Evans Picture Library; Boer War, Hulton Getty; Suffragette, Hulton Getty. Pg 12/13: Ford Model T, Hulton Getty; George V Hulton Getty; World War I, Hulton Getty; Alcock and Brown, Hulton Getty; Lenin, Hulton Getty; The Jazz Singer, Ronald Grant Archive; Boris Karloff Frankenstein, Ronald Grant Archive; Nazi rally, Hulton Getty; Chairman Mao, Corbis. Pg 15 John Galsworthy, Hulton Getty; Pg 16 John Galsworthy, Hulton Getty; Pg 17 Ada Galsworthy, Hulton Getty; Pg 18 Joseph Conrad, Hulton Getty; Pg 21 Ford Madox Ford, Hulton Getty; Pg 23 Galsworthy family, University of Birmingham Special Collection; Pg 24 Margaret Morris, Topham Picture Library; The Skin Game programme, Mander and Mitchenson Theatre Collection; Pg 29 Virginia Woolf, Hulton Getty; Pg 31 John and Ada Galsworthy, Hulton Getty; Pg 33 and 34 © Pictorial Press

All other photographs © Granada Media Group:

Set photographs taken by Stephen Fineran
Costume photographs taken by Phoebe de Gaye
Costume sketches by Phoebe de Gaye
Other photography by: Neil Marland (Stills Photographer Granada), Rachel Joseph, Carl Royle, Nicky Johnstone and Brian Moody.
Behind the scenes photographs (at the ball) were taken by Neil Marland for What's On TV Magazine and TV Quick.

Design: Simon Buchanan
Art Director: Jeremy Southgate

ISBN 0 233 05042 6

Printed and bound in Italy
10 9 8 7 6 5 4 3 2 1

CONTENTS

FOREWORD

BY SITA WILLIAMS

Sita Williams, the
series producer.

I've been living with the Forsytes for two years now, during which time I've come to feel like a member of the family – with all that entails. Families fight, they fall out, they laugh, eat, sleep and cry together. Any television producer who's ever undertaken a large-scale period drama will understand that there's been an awful lot of all of those things in the last few months. Now, however, it's satisfying to know that the Forsyte family is out there winning new friends and admirers, upsetting and inspiring and entertaining a new generation just as it has done for the last 100 years. And it will continue to do so long after this series has aired, as we will be adapting *To Let*, the third book in the saga, which tells Jon and Fleur's story – Irene and Young Jolyon's son and Soames and Annette's daughter. We plan to transmit sometime next year.

What we've tried to achieve with this book is to show that *The Forsyte Saga* is much more than just a piece of television, or a series of novels.

The books, and their author John Galsworthy, are deeply embedded in their times, and say a great deal to modern audiences not only about a crucial piece of our history but also about how far we've come in the last century. Galsworthy was a pivotal figure – on the one hand he was very much the Victorian gentleman from the stiff-upper-lip school, part of a large, prosperous family that upheld the Empire, but on the other hand he was a black sheep, a rebel against the very class that created him. To find out more about Galsworthy is to deepen an understanding of what he created. It comes, perhaps, as a shock to discover that Galsworthy considered himself a socialist and a feminist – certainly not a political radical in either of those causes, but prepared to stand up to prevailing opinion whenever his conscience prompted him. It's even more surprising to discover that Galsworthy, whom Virginia Woolf dismissed as a sexless 'stuffed shirt', scandalised his family by having an affair with a married woman, living in sin with her and throwing away his humdrum career in law as a direct result.

But that's typical of Galsworthy and the Forsytes. They look so respectable on the surface, with all those gleaming white shirt fronts, those immaculate hairdos and elegant dresses, but underneath the façade there are just the same passions, the same intrigues and the same venal impulses that are no respecters of class. Galsworthy revealed those things with a gentle, humorous and understanding touch – he played equally well in the comic and the tragic vein.

Anyone who has read the Forsyte novels will know that you're about to meet an awful lot of new people all at once, and that it will take a little time to get used to them and their ways. This book will help you to understand a little of what makes the Forsytes tick, to figure out who's who and to see just why the two halves of the family always seem to be at daggers drawn. But be warned: if you don't want to know what happens in the TV adaptation, you should proceed with caution. Plot details are revealed, and this is a saga that's full of surprises!

Sita Williams

Controlled chaos in the magnificent ballroom at Knowsley House. The director, Chris Menaul, gives instructions to Gina McKee while Ben Miles adjusts his neckwear.

JOHN GALSWORTHY

HIS LIFE AND TIMES

THE FORSYTE SAGA IS THE PRODUCT OF A
PIVOTAL TIME IN ENGLISH HISTORY, WHEN
THE CERTAINTIES OF THE EMPIRE WERE
CRUMBLING WITH THE ADVENT OF THE
MODERN AGE. JOHN GALSWORTHY WAS AT
THE CENTRE OF THE STORM – A WRITER
DEEPLY ROOTED IN VICTORIANISM, BUT
WITH AN EYE TO THE FUTURE.

CHRONOLOGY

1867
Karl Marx publishes the first volume of *Das Kapital*.
John Galsworthy born 14 August in Coombe, near Kingston, Surrey.

1868
Gladstone becomes prime minister. Wilkie Collins's *The Moonstone*.

1867 Karl Marx

1870
Franco-Prussian War.

1871
George Eliot *Middlemarch*.

1880 The First Boer War

1880
First Boer War starts, Gladstone PM.

1881
Henrik Ibsen *Ghosts*, first public electricity supply in Godalming, Surrey.
Galsworthy goes to Harrow.

1887
Queen Victoria's Golden Jubilee, radio waves demonstrated.

1888
Wilhelm II becomes emperor of Germany.

1889
Graduates from Oxford.

1890
Called to the Bar.

1891
Meets Ada Pearson Cooper, newly married to his cousin, Arthur.

1897
Queen Victoria's Diamond Jubilee, aspirin marketed for the first time.
Publishes first book of short stories, *From the Four Winds*.

1898
H G Wells *The War of the Worlds*.
Publishes first novel, *Jocelyn*, and travels to Italy with Ada.

1899
Second Boer War, Boxer rising, Sigmund Freud *The Interpretation of Dreams*.

1900
Relief of Mafeking, Joseph Conrad *Lord Jim*, Giacomo Puccini *Tosca*.
Publishes *Villa Rubein*, a novel, and meets Ford Madox Ford and Edward Garnett.

1901
Death of Queen Victoria, Edward VII becomes king.
Publishes *A Man of Devon*, a volume of short stories that contains the first Forsyte characters.

Emily Pankhurst i
arrested, 1903

1872

1873
Leo Tolstoy *Anna Karenina*.

1874
Disraeli becomes PM, first Impressionist exhibition.

1875

1876
Bell patents first telephone.

1884
Galsworthy Captains the house football XI.

1901 Edward VII becomes king

1885
Lord Salisbury PM, first Benz motor car, Emile Zola *Germinal*.

1886
Gladstone PM, resigns over Home Rule, Salisbury PM. Thomas Hardy *The Mayor of Casterbridge*.
Galsworthy goes to Oxford to read law, action of *The Man of Property* opens.

1892
Gladstone PM.

1893
Independent Labour Party formed.
During a trip around the world meets Joseph Conrad in Adelaide.

1894
Lord Rosebery PM.

1895
Lord Salisbury PM, Lumière brothers demonstrate cinema, Oscar Wilde *The Importance of Being Earnest*.
Begins affair with Ada.

1896
Thomas Hardy *Jude the Obscure*.

1902
Balfour PM.
Ada leaves her husband.

1903
Suffragette movement in Britain, Wright brothers demonstrate powered flight.

1904
Anton Chekhov *The Cherry Orchard*.
Galsworthy's father dies. Publishes *The Island Pharisees*, a novel.

1905
First Russian Revolution, Campbell-Bannerman PM, Albert Einstein special theory of relativity.
Ada's divorce comes through, Galsworthy marries her on 23 September.

1906
Labour Party formed in Britain.
***The Man of Property*, first part of *The Forsyte Saga*, published. *The Silver Box* produced at the Court Theatre.**

1907

George Bernard Shaw *Major Barbara*, electric washing machine marketed.
Publishes *A Country House* (novel) and produces new play *Joy* at the Savoy Theatre. Forms a committee with J M Barrie to fight censorship laws.

1908

Old-age pensions introduced in Britain, Asquith PM, E M Forster *A Room with a View*, cubist movement.

1909 The Model T Ford

1909

Ford Model T car on sale.
Publishes *Fraternity* (novel) and produces *Strife* at the Duke of York's Theatre.

1910

George V becomes king, Post-Impressionist exhibition in London.
Produces *Justice* at the Duke of York's and meets Margaret Morris.

1910 George V

1911

Industrial unrest in UK.
Publishes *The Patrician* (novel) and produces *The Little Dream* and *Lords and Masters* in Manchester. Begins affair with Margaret Morris.

1917

Second Russian Revolution, battle of Paschendaele, US enters war, Franz Kafka *Metamorphosis*.
Returns from France. Refuses knighthood. Publishes *Beyond* (novel) and produces *Foundations* at the Royalty Theatre.

1918

Armistice ends World War One.
Publishes *Five Stories* (collection of short stories) and begins work on *In Chancery*, the second of the Forsyte novels. Moves to Hampstead.

1919

Sinn Fein set up parliament in Ireland, treaty of Versailles, formation of Weimar republic, Alcock and Brown fly Atlantic.
Publishes *Saint's Progress* (novel) and does a lecture tour of the United States. Publishes a satirical work, *The Burning Spear*, under a pseudonym.

1920

Prohibition in US, Marcel Duchamp *Mona Lisa*.
Publishes *In Chancery* (novel) and produces *The Skin Game* at St Martin's Theatre.

1919 Alcock and Brown

1921

Chinese Communist Party formed by Mao Zedong.
Publishes *To Let* (novel) and *The Bells of Peace* (poetry). Produces *A Family Man* at the Comedy Theatre. Becomes first president of PEN, the international writers' club.

1927

Charles Lindbergh flies Atlantic, BBC founded, Walt Disney *Mickey Mouse*, Al Jolson stars in *The Jazz Singer*, the first talkie.
Publishes *Two Forsyte Interludes* (stories).

1928

Women over 21 get the vote in the UK, penicillin discovered.
Publishes *Swan Song* (novel). Travels to Brazil.

1929

Depression begins, MacDonald PM.
Publishes *A Modern Comedy* (*The White Monkey*, *The Silver Spoon*, *Swan Song*), the second Forsyte trilogy, in a single volume. Produces *Exiled* and *The Roof* in London. Receives the Order of Merit.

1927 Al Jolson

1930

Evelyn Waugh *Vile Bodies*, first World Cup in football.
Publishes *On Forsyte 'Change* (short stories). Travels to USA for last time.

1931

Virginia Woolf *The Waves*, Boris Karloff stars in *Frankenstein*.
Publishes *Maid in Waiting*.

1931 Boris Karloff

1912

Titanic sinks, ANC formed in South Africa, Carl Jung *The Psychology of the Unconscious*.
Produces *The Pigeon* at the Royalty Theatre, and *The Eldest Son* at the Kingsway. Ends affair with Margaret Morris. Visits America with Ada.

1913

D H Lawrence *Sons and Lovers*, Marcel Proust *Du Côté de chez Swann*.
Publishes *The Dark Flower* (novel) and produces *The Fugitive* at the Royal Court Theatre. Visits Egypt.

1914

World War One starts.
Mother dies.
Produces *The Mob* in Manchester.

1914 start of the First World War

1915

Disaster at Gallipoli, *Lusitania* sunk.
Publishes *The Freelands* (novel) and produces *A Bit o' Love* at the Kingsway Theatre.

1916

Battles of Verdun, Somme and Jutland, Easter Rising in Dublin, Lloyd George PM.
Undertakes service with the Red Cross in Hôpital Bénévolé, Martouret, France.

1922

USSR formed, Mussolini forms government in Italy, Bonar Law PM, James Joyce *Ulysses*, T S Eliot *The Waste Land*.
Produces *Windows* at the Royal Court, and *Loyalties* at the St Martin's. *The Forsyte Saga* (*The Man of Property*, *In Chancery*, *To Let*) published in a single volume.

1923

Baldwin PM.
Publishes *Captures* (short stories).

1924 Death of Lenin

1924

MacDonald first Labour PM, Baldwin PM again, death of Lenin, André Breton surrealist manifesto.
Publishes *The White Monkey*, the fourth Forsyte novel. Produces *The Forest* and *Old English* at the St Martin's Theatre. Sister Lilian dies. Travels to Africa.

1925

Adolf Hitler *Mein Kampf*.
Publishes *Caravan* (short stories) and produces *The Show* at St Martin's. Travels to USA.

Chairman Mao 1921

1926

General strike in UK, first television.
Publishes *The Silver Spoon* (novel) and produces *Escape* at the Ambassador Theatre. Buys Bury House, Sussex.

1932

Oswald Mosley forms the British Union of Fascists, Cockcroft and Walton split the atom.
Publishes *Flowering Wilderness*. Receives Nobel Prize for Literature.

1933

Nazis win German elections.
Dies 31 January at Grove Lodge, Hampstead. Ashes scattered at Bury. *Over the River* (novel) published posthumously.

1934

Stalin purges begin, long march in China, Henry Miller *Tropic of Cancer*.
***The End of the Chapter* (*Maid in Waiting*, *Flowering Wilderness*, *Over the River*) published in single volume.**

1935

German Jews lose citizenship, Baldwin PM, Marx Brothers star in *A Night at the Opera*.
***Collected Poems*, edited by Ada, published.**

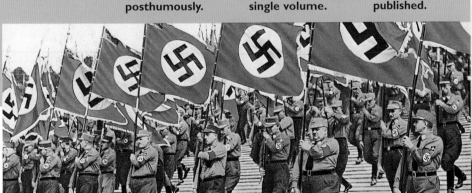

JOHN GALSWORTHY AND
THE FORSYTE SAGA

During his lifetime, John Galsworthy was the most successful writer in the business. He produced nearly thirty novels and volumes of short stories, the same number of plays, a dozen volumes of essays plus thousands of words of poetry. His books sold in vast quantities, his plays packed theatres in the West End and all over the world. He refused a knighthood, accepted the Order of Merit and a fistful of honorary degrees; in 1932, a year before his death, he was awarded the Nobel Prize for Literature.

After his death, however, Galsworthy dropped out of favour and has languished in unfashionable semi-obscurity ever since. He was too traditional for the modern writers – Virginia Woolf dismissed him as 'that stuffed shirt', D H Lawrence attacked his lack of sex – and, by the time World War Two came along, he seemed hopelessly out of date, a not so charming relic from a bygone age of doilies and tea parties. Galsworthy's world of privilege, of emotional repression – in short, the Victorian/Edwardian world – seemed silly next to the horrors of the Holocaust. Now, if he's known at all, he's associated with a very famous TV series of the 1960s.

There's a great difference, however, between a *fashionable* writer and a *good* writer. Galsworthy isn't worshipped in English literature departments, and his books will never be seen sticking out of the jacket pockets of pale young men eager to impress their peers – but that's not to say that he's not been read, steadily and with mounting appreciation, by generations of enthusiastic converts. His major novels have never been out of print, and sell enough copies to keep them in most bookshops. To some extent he's become, nearly a hundred years after his greatest success, an underground writer, passionately admired by the few but overlooked by the majority. Strangely, for a Nobel Prize-winning British author, there is at the present time no biography of Galsworthy in print, nor do most public libraries stock the handful of standard works on the subject. Even more than his contemporary Arnold Bennett, John Galsworthy dwells in a literary limbo from which his few champions have so far failed to rescue him.

Why has Galsworthy been consigned to this twilight? His world is less remote than that of Dickens, his writing more consistent than that of Lawrence, far more accessible than Woolf's. There are two answers to that question. First, there's an image problem: Galsworthy is associated too closely with the people he wrote about. Readers assume that the stuffy aunts and tight-lipped lawyers who feature in the books are actually what Galsworthy is all about, whereas in fact they were members of a class of which Galsworthy, although a member, was highly critical. Secondly, there's that TV adaptation. The BBC's 26-part series *The Forsyte Saga* became a benchmark in television drama in 1967, boosted sales of the novels and forged an eternal image of the uptight, upright Forsytes with their canes and gloves and lacy dresses. Nothing dates faster than television – and memories of the BBC's *The Forsyte Saga* contribute to the image of Galsworthy as a stuffy, creaky old writer from a bygone age.

All it would take to dispel this image is a quick dip into *The Man of Property*, the first novel in what was to become *The Forsyte Saga*. Here is writing, page after page of it, that's witty, sharp, tongue-in-cheek, suffused with an understated eroticism and bursting with originality. The cast of characters – those ancient Victorian relics still living in a glorious past while their sons and daughters make an almighty hash of the present – are as vividly drawn as anything else in the twentieth century. The dialogue is by turns elegant and wicked, a mixture of Oscar Wilde and Joe Orton. And the stories – of adultery, greed, regret, rape – are delivered with narrative mastery. To read the first few chapters of *The Forsyte Saga* is to be hooked for all nine volumes. You won't get an orgasm every ten pages, or very much violence, and precious little in the way of shopping; but, if you approach Galsworthy with an open mind, you'll get the nearest the English novel ever approached to Tolstoy, but with laughs.

The boss: Galsworthy at the height of his career, the image of prosperous conservatism.

John Galsworthy didn't take naturally to writing. For the first half of his life, he seemed inclined to do anything but: he played sports, he gambled, he trained for the Bar, he dabbled with causes, he chased women. He was born into that class of late Victorians who had no real need to work: the Galsworthys came from prosperous farming stock (they pronounced the surname with a short 'a' until the end of the nineteenth century) who had moved to London and increased their wealth through property and investment and the practice of law. When John (the fourth generation of oldest sons to bear that name) arrived, the family lived in Kingston, Surrey, in a large house with servants, horses, carriages and its own cricket pitch. In his own parlance, Galsworthy was born with a silver spoon in his mouth, and never pretended otherwise – another reason why later generations, who equate proletarian roots with literary authenticity, turned their backs on him.

Galsworthy followed the expected course through Harrow and Oxford, where he distinguished himself more as a footballer than an intellectual. He was good-looking and popular with women, enjoyed singing and socialising and, after graduating with a gentlemanly second-class degree, took the Victorian equivalent of a gap year, travelling around the world with a friend, looking for adventure, before he settled into the family firm. Travel may have broadened his horizons, but not much: young Galsworthy came home, completed his legal training and was called to the Bar in 1890. His heart wasn't in it; he missed his only chance at courtroom action because he'd been too busy chatting to his father on the steps, while a fellow barrister did his business before the judge. Unsurprisingly, he never received another brief, and whiled away his time doing legal research and opinion-writing.

This might have been the end of the story but for a meeting in 1891 that changed Galsworthy's life for ever. His cousin Arthur had just married a charming 27-year-old woman, the wonderfully named Ada Nemesis Pearson Cooper, and she was duly presented to the wider family at a series of nuptial parties. At one of these she met John. Neither thought much of the meeting at the time, but within two years John and Ada were meeting often, and within four years they had become lovers. Their relationship remained passionate and secret for over ten

Young John, Captain of the Harrow First Football XI in 1885.

years, and it was this experience that threw Galsworthy off the tracks of his Victorian upbringing and gave him the decisive push towards writing. And it wasn't just his scandalous, outsider status that drove him to art: Ada identified his talent and told him, right at the outset of their affair, that he should become a writer.

The law was making him miserable – he remained in practice only to please his parents – whereas writing (not a respectable profession, nor necessarily a lucrative one) was something of which he dreamed constantly. It was Ada who inspired, encouraged and sometimes bullied Galsworthy into putting pen to paper; there is little doubt that she believed in his talent, but she also had a taste for the kind of high life to which an established author had access. Solicitors were all very well in their way, and she'd never want for anything as the wife or lover of a Galsworthy, but Ada craved excitement and position to which literary cachet would be her passport.

Ada Galsworthy in 1913 – a respectable married woman at last.

From 1895 to 1905, Galsworthy lived in a social, professional limbo. Selected members of the family knew of his liaison with Ada, and were deeply disapproving (at least on the surface), so much so that they insisted the affair be kept secret from his father. Galsworthy braved the scandal, and travelled frequently abroad with Ada on a series of romantic holidays. It was harder to carry off at home, though: Ada remained married to Galsworthy's cousin Arthur and lived with him until 1902, while Galsworthy bore the social stigma of being a known adulterer. He was cut at his club, the Junior Carlton – but there was little he could do about it. An open scandal was just what the Galsworthys feared, and John colluded in a conspiracy of silence and keeping up of appearances. After seven years, however, it was too much – Ada left her husband and set up home with John, far from the disapproving eyes of society in Dartmoor. Galsworthy was not, perhaps, a brave man; unlike Wilkie Collins, or Elizabeth Gaskell, he was too sensitive to the morals of his time to flout them openly. He was, however, taking a decisive step beyond the pale.

He wasn't faring much better professionally. It was all very well for Ada to tell him to become a writer, and for friends such as Joseph Conrad and Ford Madox Ford to lavish praise on his early efforts, but in 1897, when he published his first volume of stories, Galsworthy was a long way from hitting his stride. *From the Four Winds* was a motley collection, published at Galsworthy's own expense under the pseudonym John Sinjohn – he was still sufficiently bound by family feeling not to 'shame' his relations with his shady literary endeavours. Conrad, whom Galsworthy had met on a boat during his gap year, when the former was still a merchant seaman, helped as much as he could, rustling up good reviews and negotiating with publishers for the first full-length novel, published by Duckworth in 1898. *Jocelyn*, a love story that reflects Galsworthy's own troubled personal life, received bad reviews and sold little – it was a flop that might have put lesser men off the whole idea of writing. Galsworthy, however, had Ada breathing down his neck, and bounced back in 1900 with another novel, *Villa Rubein*, a botched tale of love among the artists that even Galsworthy's friend Ford Madox Ford couldn't praise. 'There is not enough vinegar in the salad,' said Ford. 'You haven't enough contempt.'

Joseph Conrad, Galsworthy's greatest booster, ultimately eclipsed by his protégé's success.

Galsworthy took these words to heart, and retreated for a while to consider his direction. In this he was greatly assisted by Edward Garnett, an editor and publisher's reader who provided the very thing that Galsworthy needed: a friendly but critical mentor, someone who could teach rather than simply praise, in short the missing vinegar in the Galsworthian salad. Garnett could rise to heights of rudeness, and Galsworthy was sensible enough to listen; soon he was writing a short story about a character called Swithin Forsyte, and planning the novel that was to become *The Man of Property*.

The year 1904 was the end of the beginning. Galsworthy published his last journey-man work, *The Island Pharisees* – the first to show any real critical/satirical spirit, and the first to be published under his own name. It's no coincidence that 1904 also saw the death of John Galsworthy Sr, thus liberating his son from the need for personal secrecy and professional circumspection. Freudian psychoanalysts could have a field day with Galsworthy – for it was only with the death of his father that he unleashed his real powers as a writer, and sorted out his messy personal life. Daddy died in December; wasting no time, John and Ada openly set up house together, went through the rigmarole of being caught in the act by a private detective, and were served with divorce papers. The family closed ranks, there was as little scandal as possible (cousin Arthur, by all accounts, was not popular), and the divorce was done by September. John and Ada celebrated the decree absolute by getting married on the very day it arrived. It was a very small, private ceremony.

More significantly, Galsworthy got to work on the novel upon which his subsequent fame rests. *The Man of Property* was begun in 1903, 'at the time of my life most poignant', and it took Galsworthy three years to complete. During that time he had lost his father and married Ada – Galsworthy, like many a writer before and since, needed the spur of personal trauma to bring his talents to life. 'It was written here, there and everywhere,' he said, 'the most scattered of my manuscripts … I knew it to be the best I had written; and the revision of it, sentence by sentence, gave me more intimate pleasure than I am likely to have again.'[1] Galsworthy polished the manuscript right up to its publication in 1906, entertaining grand ideas of its significance (he almost subtitled it 'National Ethics' or 'Tales of a Christian People', but thought better of it).

The Man of Property was a success – the first real success that Galsworthy had tasted, although only a hint of what was to come. It was widely and well reviewed, enjoyed brisk sales and brought its author to the attention of the press (much to the jealousy of Galsworthy's former mentors Conrad and Ford, who realised that their young pet was about to become more famous than they were). Galsworthy, for once, had his finger directly on the pulse. He knew intimately the people he was writing about, he'd served up a well-made salad with just the right amount of vinegar, and he'd hit upon the very issues that were the staple of national conversation: marriage, money, divorce, adultery. The novel opens in 1886, but, for all its historical gloss, it's a contemporary story, even rather daring in its direct discussion of marital relations. And, in the Forsyte family, Galsworthy had identified a national archetype, a group of people that everybody knew and loved – or hated. This was no coincidence. More than ever before, Galsworthy was writing about his own family.

To understand *The Man of Property* is to understand Galsworthy. It's a novel that is at once of a certain social class, and fiercely critical of that class. It's written by an insider, a man so far steeped in the Forsyte code that he can never truly escape it, who is at the same time a spy in the camp. Galsworthy satirised his own class, but never lost sight

[1] Draft speech for Nobel Prize ceremony, 1932, quoted in Catherine Dupré, *John Galsworthy*.

of the fact that there was as much to be praised in them as condemned. Soames Forsyte, the 'man of property' himself, the man who puts social standing and financial expedience above all else, who represses his passions so far that they become twisted and violent, is also a man of tenderness, insight and resolve. He'd be useless as a confidant, but, in the event of a crisis, he's the one you'd want to have around. And for Galsworthy – as for his readers – to know someone intimately, faults and all, is to understand and even love him.

Soames stands at a social crossroads. His family – all those uncles and aunts in Park Lane, his kindly but hidebound parents – represent the old order, the empire builders, so sure in their beliefs that nothing can ever really touch them. Beyond Soames is a world that he can never fully understand – the new world where feelings and spontaneity count more than property and respectability, where art has an intrinsic value beyond its market price. Soames is a collector – of paintings, of properties, of people. He sees his wife, Irene, primarily as a good investment, a beautiful woman who will be good for his social standing and who will provide sons to continue the family line.

But there's more to Soames than that. While his surface is impeccably Victorian, his inner self is in a very modern turmoil. He adores Irene passionately, sexually, but can never express it to her. He despises the straitjacket of family values, even ridicules his foolish relatives, but would never dream of offending them. Galsworthy's later critics took Soames (and his creator) at face value, wanting him to be only one thing or the other. They mistook the trappings of the novel for its meaning, and dismissed it as bourgeois propaganda. It's anything but. *The Man of Property* shows the tragic results of social convention and financial greed – but Galsworthy was too subtle a writer to hit his reader over the head with his 'meaning'. He saw in his characters, in his life, in himself, an indissoluble mixture of good and bad. In this he was more modern than the moderns. 'Life,' said Guy de Maupassant, 'is never as good or as bad as one believes' – and it was this daringly French dictum that Galsworthy applied to English fiction. Beside his witty, subtle portraits, the blunt polemics of Lawrence and the miasmal doodlings of Woolf look insubstantial and naïve.

Now that Galsworthy was writing under his own name and attracting a good deal of public attention, the family got the jitters. His older sister Lilian, reading the manuscript before publication, advised her brother that he would upset his relatives and reopen the scandal of his relationship with Ada. There was no doubt in Lilian's mind that the portrait of a marriage in *The Man of Property* drew directly on Ada's unhappy relationship with cousin Arthur. Surely, she urged, he should withdraw under the shelter of a pseudonym, just as he had done before. Galsworthy replied in very un-Soamesian style.

'Apart from you, Mab [his younger sister] and Mother (who perhaps had better not read the book) who really knows enough or takes enough interest in us to make it more than a two days wonder that I should choose such a subject? Who knows enough even to connect A [Ada] with I [Irene], especially as I have changed her hair to gold?'[2]

This was disingenuous on Galsworthy's part. Of course he would embarrass his family, and of course people would point at Ada as the model for Irene, whatever colour he dyed her hair. What he's saying, in characteristically bluff terms, is that he doesn't give a damn what the family thinks – he's made his break and is going, henceforth, to be an artist. The fact that the book was a great success, and brought a good deal of glory to the family name, must have softened the blow for Lilian, Mab and Mother.

The Man of Property was not conceived as the first part of a series of novels. Galsworthy recognised its potential quickly, and even before publication he was writing to Edward Garnett about the possibility of some sequels, although the plots he outlined in 1906 were never executed. But he had other fish to fry – and the world wouldn't hear from the Forsyte family for another fourteen years. A good deal happened in between: Galsworthy became a successful dramatist, campaigned on every social issue under the sun, almost destroyed his marriage and underwent the great upheaval of World War One. But it may be worth jumping ahead at this point to consider what exactly makes up *The Forsyte Saga*, and those books sometimes erroneously included under that title.

Ford Madox Ford: 'I think I must have been the first person really to take Galsworthy seriously as a writer.'

Galsworthy revived Soames and Irene in 1920 with *In Chancery*, a sequel to *The Man of Property*. The book had been conceived at the end of the war; half a dozen other

[2] Quoted Dupré, p. 111.

novels and several hit plays had intervened. It's not as if Galsworthy's inspiration was flagging – he was at the height of his success – but there's no doubt that he recognised the Forsytes as his greatest literary invention. 'I think the July Sunday at Wingstone in 1918, when it suddenly came to me that I could go on with my Forsytes … was the happiest day of my writing life,' he said when the book was published.[3] With the completion of *In Chancery*, Galsworthy took only a couple of weeks' break before steaming ahead with *To Let*, the last part of what he then saw as a trilogy, bringing to a close the story of Soames and Irene and showing their tragedy echoed in the fortunes of their children.

To Let was published in 1921, and in May of the following year all three books came out in one volume under the general heading *The Forsyte Saga*. It was at this point that the sales really took off, and Galsworthy's publishers realised that a Forsyte novel was a guaranteed bestseller. Galsworthy would go on to write a further six books dealing with the family, the final one completed just before his death in 1933 and published posthumously, and these, alongside the first three, are officially known as *The Forsyte Chronicles*. The second trilogy (*The White Monkey*, *Silver Spoon* and *Swan Song*) appeared between 1924 and 1928, and in a single volume as *A Modern Comedy* in 1929. *The End of the Chapter*, the last trilogy, comprised *Maid in Waiting*, *The Flowering Wilderness* and *Over the River*. Nine novels, three trilogies, one *Chronicles*. There was no masterplan: Galsworthy just got the bit between his teeth and carried on writing till he dropped.

The Forsyte Saga contains the story of Soames, Irene and her lover Bosinney, and it's the first two books, *The Man of Property* and *In Chancery*, that provide the material for the new ITV adaptation. That trilogy concludes with *To Let*, containing the story of Soames's daughter Fleur (by his second marriage, to Annette) and Irene's son Jon (by her second marriage, to Jolyon), how they fall in love and are ultimately forced apart by family history.

A Modern Comedy puts Fleur once more centre stage. She's now married to the likable young publisher Michael Mont, but it's an unsettled liaison constantly threatened by her unquenched love for young Jon. Soames features as an important secondary character, detached from the action for much of the time, perplexed by his daughter's waywardness until the very end, when he steps in decisively and with disastrous results.

The End of the Chapter breaks yet further from the original set of characters. It's now 1928, and the action focuses on Dinny Charwell, a thoroughly modern young woman who does pretty much as she pleases, speaks her mind and even drives a car. It's the lightest and funniest of the three trilogies, and it shows Galsworthy writing with almost careless brilliance. Most of the critical works on the subject dismiss *The End of the*

[3] To Harley Granville Barker, quoted in Dupré, p. 254.

Chapter, and much of *A Modern Comedy*, as potboilers (some, in fact, insist that Galsworthy's talent was all used up in *The Man of Property*). But the characters are as lively as ever, even more so in the case of Dinny and her great aunt, Em, the benign progeny of Mrs Malaprop and Lady Bracknell. Galsworthy was softened by success, perhaps, no longer the angry young man who poured all his disillusionment with his class into *The Forsyte Saga*. He was rich and successful and happy, and that's reflected in his later work. But the *Chronicles* do not end on a downbeat note. His concern is still with love and marriage, money and morals, but he handles it this time with a lightness and a resignation that make delightful reading.

The fourteen years between *The Man of Property* and *In Chancery* saw Galsworthy undergoing some kind of midlife crisis. This was as much to do with the times in which he lived as with any personal considerations – it was impossible for anyone to live through World War One without questioning all the beliefs and assumptions they'd been brought up with. But for Galsworthy, it was a traumatic period on all fronts. *The Man of Property*, and marriage to Ada, eased him into his forties as a respected artist and a respectable member of society. It would have been easy to rest on his laurels, and turn

The Galsworthys. Centre: Blanche and John Galsworthy snr. Far left: Mabel; seated right: Lilian; John is standing behind her.

out more popular books, but Galsworthy had ambitions beyond literary fiction. He had causes – dozens of causes – and discovered that the most effective and direct way of addressing them was in the theatre. To this end he wrote a play exposing the English class divide entitled *The Silver Box*, got it produced at the Court Theatre and found himself instantly established as a hit dramatist. For the next ten years, Galsworthy's energies were divided equally between the theatre and the novel.

The theatre brought Galsworthy his most intense professional acclaim; it also led him into the depths of despair. It was during the preparation of his play *The Little Dream* in 1910 that Galsworthy met a young 'expressive dancer', Margaret Morris, at the Savoy Theatre. He was 44, rich and married; she was 19, impressionable and very beautiful. Galsworthy took, at first, a professional interest in her, got her a job in *The Little Dream* and even helped her to set up a school of dance and movement. Ada, also, took the dreamy young girl under her wing, and presumably viewed her as just another of Jack's pet causes, albeit a dangerously attractive one. Margaret, for her part, fell deeply in love with Galsworthy, and poured out her feelings across dozens of pages of diaries and letters in which she squirmed in frustration at Galsworthy's lack of response. The great writer, perceptive in so many things, had a blind spot where

Margaret Morris was concerned, and failed to realise the effect he was having on her – or perhaps he knew all too well, but, being aware of the terrible effects it could have on his marriage, chose to ignore it. Eventually, however, the pretence dropped, and Galsworthy took what was so manifestly on offer. Nobody knows just what he took: Ada, in later years, exercised a strict control over biographical material relating to her husband, and the most we can be sure of is that the guilty couple shared a kiss and a cuddle in the back of a taxi. For this we have Margaret Morris's word. Whether it went any further than that is a matter of pure speculation – but, whether their love remained on a platonic level or otherwise, it tore Ada to pieces and plunged her into depression and ill health. Galsworthy, after nearly two years of desperate self-analysis, dumped Margaret by means of a letter, and fled with Ada to France.

This episode has been used by Galsworthy's detractors to show what a cold fish he was, and indeed there's nothing admirable in his treatment of his lover. But it's hard to judge him, even so. Of course he was attracted by Margaret, and flattered by her attentions – and she was relentless in her pursuit. It seems that the Galsworthys' sex life was humdrum and infrequent; Ada, by all accounts, was not a passionate woman, and one of the reasons for her hatred of her first husband was his 'coarseness' in the bedroom. Galsworthy spared her all that, and didn't push his conjugal rights – no Soames Forsyte he. Occasionally she relented and allowed him into her bed, and Galsworthy marked the event with a capital 'A' in his diary. They never had children. Most men of Galsworthy's class would have accepted this, and kept a couple of mistresses on the side.

Not Galsworthy. When temptation came, he was too much the man of principle to enjoy a quick fling behind his wife's back. He and Ada had always shared a belief in free love, a belief forged, no doubt, in the difficult years of her bondage to a husband she hated. Man and woman should love one another without the force of law holding them together. This was all well and fine in theory, but the practice was a different matter. When Ada found out about Galsworthy's feelings (he told her, of course) she became physically ill with jealousy, a martyr to his inappropriate passions. Galsworthy cared too much about Ada, whom he loved with the utmost devotion, to see her suffer in this way. His was not a pragmatic approach to marriage, but it was an honest one. The fact that none of the parties got what they wanted out of this emotional entanglement just served to highlight the absurdity of Galsworthy's high-mindedness. Absurd it may have been, but it reveals him as a man of passion and an almost fanatical honesty, certainly not a cold fish.

After the Margaret Morris affair, Galsworthy schooled himself in a reticence of which Soames Forsyte would have been proud. Even close family members recorded

Margaret Morris, the 'expressive dancer' who precipitated a crisis in Galsworthy's marriage.

his reluctance to discuss private matters ('Books we could discuss, feelings, no,' wrote his niece, Dorothy Easton), and it seems that the only outlet for Galsworthy's repressed emotional life was his pets. Throughout their married life, John and Ada kept a succession of dogs, upon whom they lavished all the affection that other couples gave to their children. Ada even wrote a memoir of the Galsworthy hounds, entitled *The Dear Dogs*. The most cherished of these companions, the spaniel Chris, died in 1911, leaving Ada 'prostrate' with grief. Some of the most moving passages in *The Forsyte Chronicles* deal with animals – the love of dogs, and the relief of their uncomplicated affection, was a characteristic of the older Soames, and the older Galsworthy.

It was against this rocky background that Galsworthy established himself as one of England's most successful writers and public figures. His theatrical career gave him a profile that fiction alone could never achieve, for it put him at the forefront of an intellectual and social movement – the very place where he wanted to be. In this Galsworthy was lucky. The 'theatre of ideas', spearheaded by socially conscious writers such as Henrik Ibsen and George Bernard Shaw, was putting serious debate onto the stage, sweeping away the drawing room comedies of the recent past. Stage plays were still censored (they would remain so, despite the efforts of Galsworthy and a few others, until 1968), and it was difficult to introduce anything really contentious into popular drama, but writers were trying their best. Ibsen's plays, which discussed adultery, feminism and even syphilis, were performed at first under club conditions (thus escaping censorship), and acted as a clarion call to British dramatists to follow suit. Shaw waded in with shocking plays such as *Mrs Warren's Profession* (prostitution), and Galsworthy was quick to follow suit. *The Silver Box* was the story of two men, one rich, one poor, in trouble with the law for much the same misdemeanour, and traced the disparity in their fate. *Strife* (1909) tackled industrial relations, and *Justice*, later the same year, protested against the inhumanities of the penal system. On stage, Galsworthy was more argumentative, more propagandist; he reserved his dissection of the subtleties of life for his novels. The novels are a nocturne in various shades of grey; the stage plays are bold designs in black and white.

This approach worked. To Galsworthy's delight, *Justice* led directly to a review of the practice, then universal, of putting all prisoners directly into solitary confinement. With this encouragement, he couldn't adopt causes quickly enough. Galsworthy wrote down a list of 22 personal crusades that included 'Abolition of the Censorship of plays, Sweated industries, Minimum wage, Labour exchanges, women's suffrage, ponies in mines, Divorce Law Reform, Docking of Horses' Tails, Slaughterhouse reform, Plumage bill, Slum clearance, Children on the stage'. This was no idle dilettantism: Galsworthy

ST MARTIN'S THEATRE
THE SKIN GAME

would muck in with all of the above, famously visiting a series of notorious abattoirs and getting up to his elbows in blood.

The idea of Galsworthy as a political writer may seem ridiculous to those who know his work only through *The Forsyte Saga*, or through the TV adaptation, but the vein of political radicalism runs right throughout his writing. The plays are the most obvious example, but even in *The Man of Property* Galsworthy is chipping away at the establishment, albeit with the subtler weapons of satire. But there is no doubt that he was serious in his support of feminism, and sympathised with the early ideals of socialism. By the time of *The End of the Chapter* he was writing openly about soup kitchens, and introducing well-rounded working-class figures into his fiction. True, he was no George Orwell – his sympathies were too broad for that. But Galsworthy was certainly an outspoken champion of anyone he perceived to be an underdog, even if he did most of his campaigning from the comfort of his various splendid homes.

It was World War One more than anything else that shook Galsworthy out of the final vestiges of his Victorian upbringing. It was the end of the world that he had written about, the end of Forsytism in its purest form, although Galsworthy, like the Forsytes, would survive and even flourish in the changed landscape of 1918. But for Galsworthy the war was far more than just a social change: he was utterly horrified by the *idea* of war, of slaughter, of violence. His conscience recoiled against it. This was a man who would cry over the death of a dog, who would campaign vigorously against the docking of horses' tails; it's not hard to imagine his reaction to the horrors of the trenches. Even before the war news became the protracted nightmare that began with Ypres and the Somme, Galsworthy was desperate to do something – almost anything – to help. He wanted to volunteer, of course, but he was too old (47) and far too short-sighted to be accepted for active service. Undaunted, he contributed to the running of ambulances, and gave generous cash gifts for the comfort of British soldiers travelling to France.

But this was not enough: Galsworthy could not sit idle at home while a generation was meeting its death on the continent. In 1916 he took a course in massage, and travelled with Ada to a military hospital in the French Alps, where he worked as masseur and bathman while she attended to the linen. They stayed for a few months until exhaustion forced them home – but the experience seems to have been therapeutic, not just for the guilt-torn Galsworthys, but also to the injured and shell-shocked soldiers for whom they cared. John and Ada came home in March 1917, and spent the rest of the war in a kind of agonised stasis.

When peace came at long last, Galsworthy did what few could have predicted: he returned to the Forsytes. It was in 1918 that he had the 'revelation' of writing *In Chancery* and the remaining seven books – and this was a decisive point in his career. While the rest of European art and letters was plunging into a vortex of experimentation, Galsworthy chose to stick to the traditional literary values of which he had already proved himself a master. It is this factor perhaps above all others that underlies Galsworthy's parlous reputation in English literary history. At a time when James Joyce was remaking the novel with *Ulysses*, and T S Eliot was between *Prufrock* and *The Waste Land*, Galsworthy swam deliberately against the tide of modernism and produced *In Chancery*. The modern movement features in *The Forsyte Chronicles* – Soames collects Impressionist and Post-Impressionist art, and June runs a modern art gallery – but the writing itself, the structure and the language of the books, remains resolutely Edwardian.

Virginia Woolf, who was just starting out as a novelist in 1918, dismissed Galsworthy and Arnold Bennett as 'Edwardians', irrelevant in the brave new postwar Georgian world. 'To go to these men and ask them to teach you how to write a novel – how to create characters that are real – is precisely like going to a bootmaker and asking him to teach you how to make a watch,' she wrote in 1924, and too many subsequent critics have been quick to fall into line behind her. What Woolf wanted was the inside of the character, the ebb and flow of consciousness, not the exterior facets that, she felt, were all that Galsworthy gave. In this, of course, she was wrong: *To Let*, with its final passage of reflection from Soames, was as fine a piece of 'interior' writing as Woolf ever achieved. It must be left to individual readers to decide which school of writing, Galsworthy's or Woolf's, has worn better in the ensuing decades.

Whatever Mrs Woolf had to say about the matter, Galsworthy's career and reputation during his lifetime went from strength to strength. There were several more successful plays, including *The Skin Game* (1920), the one most worthy of revival. There were various volumes of essays, poems and short stories, although Galsworthy restricted his full-length fiction almost exclusively to Forsyte matters after 1920, recognising that the novels were 'my passport to permanency'.

After the disruptions of the Margaret Morris affair and the war, John and Ada settled into a harmonious middle age, travelling around the world, living in some style in Hampstead and Sussex, enjoying the fruits of their labours. Galsworthy, who had refused a knighthood during the war, was awarded the Order of Merit in 1929, and ruled at the head of his profession as the president of PEN, the international writers' club. The Nobel Prize came almost too late in 1932, and Galsworthy was too ill to attend the ceremony in Stockholm.

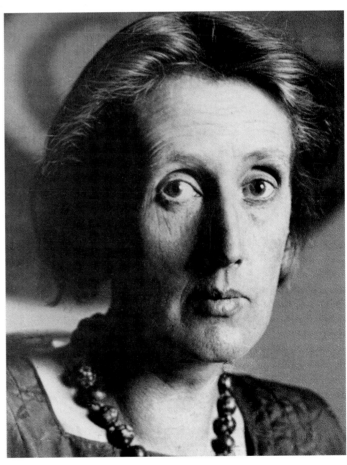

Virginia Woolf regarded Galsworthy as a 'stuffed shirt' and regularly reviled his writing.

Galsworthy's last years were a long, painful twilight. His health failed towards the end of the 1920s, and, although he kept writing, it was without the vigour that had sustained him through the previous decades. He became melancholy and prone to depression, dogged by a sense of artistic failure, presumably not helped by the critical tide that was turning against him. His love for Ada became another source of guilt: if he were to die, who would look after her? They had relied on each other for so long, been so much to each other, hurt each other and kissed it better for nearly forty years, that the idea of life for one without the other was quite unthinkable. And yet Galsworthy continued to fade. Finally, after a grim final month, Galsworthy died on 31 January 1933 at the age of 65, possibly of a brain tumour, although the causes were never certain. Ada lived on for another twenty years, tending the flame of Galsworthy's reputation, keeping the biographers at bay.

Galsworthy's legacy is hard to assess. Certainly he belongs to the great tradition of English literature; he saw himself, not unjustifiably, following a line from Thackeray and Fielding. He did not innovate, either in form or content, and has thus never been considered an artist of the first rank – but he should not be dismissed merely as a competent craftsman. He found the style that suited him, and he did it incomparably well through four decades of work. In Galsworthy's writing, and in his Forsyte novels in particular, we gain an insight into the soul of a generation that has been all but forgotten, wiped out in the Stalinist rewriting of critical history that followed the modern movement. Galsworthy, more than any English writer, captured the transitional phase of society between the certainties of the Victorian era and the frighteningly rapid change of the twentieth century. True, his vision was circumscribed; he seldom stepped outside London and the Home Counties, and was most at home writing about the upper middle classes. But his eye for detail was true, his gift of dialogue exquisite and his emotional connection with his work always honest. The treatment of Soames Forsyte, the almost-hated man of property of the early years, shows a writer maturing with his work, changing his attitudes as the world changes around him. By the time Galsworthy wrote *The White Monkey*, Soames had become a lovable, revered figure, a symbol of much that was good about an age that was rapidly disappearing. Galsworthy, as ever, could see the good and the bad in all things.

In his working methods, Galsworthy was more the tortoise than the hare. He wrote steadily for several hours, and seems not to have had much truck with the idea of 'inspiration'. Unlike his younger rivals, he did not toss off streams of consciousness, or write in a state of rapture: he planned and polished, ordered and observed. Ada noted that her husband was always taking notes, even in social situations. One night at the theatre, catching her husband staring at a woman in the audience, Ada leaned over to a friend and said, 'Jack's at work.' He drew inspiration from the world that he knew, and transformed it by the power of his imagination into fiction that has stood the test of time. The fact that he never strove after fashion or innovation means that his writing seems as fresh now as the day it was published.

And he was no fool. For all his campaigning, his politics, his war work and then after

the war with PEN, Galsworthy remained honest about the pleasure that his work brought him. He was accosted once at a party given by Winston Churchill's mother, and asked by a fellow guest, Eddie Marsh, to explain his work.

Ada and John at home in Bury, Sussex, circa 1930.

> *'If the Archangel Gabriel came down from heaven and gave you your choice, that your play should transform the prison system and be forgotten, or have no practical effect whatever and be a classic a hundred years hence, which would you choose?' Galsworthy did not answer at once, and his neighbour, who had fancied him more of a philanthropist than an artist ... was impressed by his candour when he finally opted for the classic a hundred years hence.*[4]

So much for Galsworthy as the grim-faced do-gooder, more interested in causes than art. And then there's the vexed question of his notorious emotional repression, of *The Forsyte Saga* as an epic of frustration. Again, Galsworthy knew exactly what he was doing, and summed up his work in a couple of sentences that might serve as a good key to those coming to it for the first time: 'It might be said of Shaw's plays that he creates characters who express feelings which they have not got. It might be said of mine, that I create characters who have feelings that they cannot express.'

And there, in the gap between the feeling and its expression, between the reality and the appearance, lies all that is compelling, hilarious and tragic about *The Forsyte Saga*.

[4] Christopher Hassell in his biography of Edward Marsh. Dupré, p. 154.

THE BBC ADAPTATION

It all started on 5 January 1967, when the lucky few who had access to BBC2 tuned in to the first episode of what was to become the most talked-about TV show of its generation. *The Forsyte Saga*, produced and adapted in 26 parts by Donald Wilson, was one of those rare television shows that became an event, a phenomenon. Six million viewers were regularly watching the Saturday night transmissions, making it by far the infant channel's biggest hit to date. When it was repeated on BBC1 the following year, audiences rose to 18 million for the Sunday night slot. Vicars and publicans complained that they might as well shut up shop, as everyone was staying at home to catch up on the latest instalment of Forsyte family intrigue.

The series was sold all over the world, becoming one of the BBC's first international syndication hits, and was ultimately seen by an estimated global audience of 160 million.

Television, in those days, was a very different place. There was less competition, for one thing, and even in 1967 there were still plenty of homes that did not possess a single TV, let alone one in every room. *The Forsyte Saga* launched into an arena dominated on the one hand by light entertainment (BBC1) or self-consciously highbrow material (BBC2). In its first few weeks, the show was scheduled directly against *The Black and White Minstrel Show*, then against *The Rolf Harris Show*, on which Sandy Shaw debuted her songs for Europe that would lead to a cracking Eurovision victory with 'Puppet on a String'. (*The Eurovision Song Contest* itself, in April 1967, was carefully scheduled just after *The Forsyte Saga* had finished on the other side). Elsewhere in the schedules *Doctor Who* (Patrick Troughton) was battling the cybermen, *Z Cars* was in its heyday and *The Monkees* were cutting a swathe through teenage audiences up and down the country.

In such a landscape, it's hardly surprising that *The Forsyte Saga* stood out. BBC2 had shown literary adaptations before – it was one of the channel's stated aims to deliver costume drama to its audience – but there had never been anything of the scope or audacity of *The Forsyte Saga*. The casting alone was a statement of purpose: Eric Porter (Soames), Margaret Tyzack (Winifred) and Nyree Dawn Porter (Irene) were names to be reckoned with at that time. Susan Hampshire, an unknown actress when she took on the role of Soames's daughter Fleur, became a star as a result of the series and has sustained a lengthy career on those firm foundations.

In many ways, *The Forsyte Saga* redrew the map of British broadcasting. For one thing, it was the force that drove BBC2 into many homes. When the show started, only

Eric Porter as
Soames and Nyree
Dawn Porter as
Irene.

seven million homes could receive the channel, forcing then-controller David Attenborough to explain the scheduling decision in the pages of *Radio Times*. 'BBC2 started off to provide a contrast with BBC1,' he explained, before promising that 'by the end of the year nearly 70% of homes will be in range of our broadcasting'. That increased supply was buoyed up by an increased demand – created largely by *The Forsyte Saga*.

The show's other important contribution to TV history was its treatment of 'adult' subject matter in a way that television had hitherto avoided. There was no getting around the fact that Soames raped his wife, or that she had been unfaithful, and these shocking events were discussed and debated up and down the land. BBC2 played a clever hand: Galsworthy was such an eminently respectable writer, and the drama was set in the safe, distant past, and therefore there could be no doubting the seriousness of such a drama. Had the costumes been mini-skirts and Beatle Boots, the corporation would have left itself open to accusations of sensationalism in an environment in which the views of Mary Whitehouse were not seen as particularly far out.

Donald Wilson's adaptation was hugely ambitious, covering six of the nine Forsyte novels and bringing in material from some of the 'apocrypha', the occasional short stories

Galsworthy collected under the title *On Forsyte 'Change*. Over 26 weeks, and in just over 21 hours of screen time, it journeyed into every nook and cranny of the Forsyte world, introducing cousins and uncles that only make fleeting appearances on the printed page. In conception, it was something between a costume drama and a soap opera. There

Lana Morris as Hélène and Kenneth More as Young Jolyon.

would never be anything quite like it again; the next TV generation divided those two genres more strictly. Now, we have *EastEnders* and *Coronation Street* on the one hand, *Pride and Prejudice* and *The Forsyte Saga* on the other. Long-running series, like *The Bill* or *Casualty*, are nearly always contemporary.

The Forsyte effect is most obvious in the unstinting appetite for literary adaptations, which continue to send TV producers scuttling off to the 'Eng. Lit.' shelves of their local library in search of new, unadapted properties. But, strip away the costumes, and the influence is everywhere. *The Forsyte Saga* introduced serious subject matter to the long-running serial – without it we might not see *EastEnders* dealing with marital rape as naturally as it has recently done. The success of the show in the States (where it was once shown in its entirety in one session) led producers to develop new, extended formats for high-profile series, thus giving birth to the miniseries and to the Byzantine family dramas of *Dallas* and *Dynasty*.

In the UK, *The Forsyte Saga* was the benchmark by which all other TV drama was judged, at least for 15 years. The generation that grew up watching Kenneth More, Nyree Dawn Porter and Susan Hampshire created an avid audience for the classic drama serials of the 70s and 80s, for shows like *The Onedin Line*, *The Pallisers*, *Upstairs Downstairs* and *The Duchess of Duke Street*. It was only when a new, post-Forsyte audience grew to adulthood that the genre was dusted off and retooled to give us the slick, cinematic treatments that mark the best of the bunch in the 90s and 00s.

There will, of course, be comparisons made between the 1967 production and the 2002 Granada version, which is unfair but inevitable. There would not have been the one without the other. But, just as Donald Wilson's ambitious adaptation of 1967 said as much about the 1960s as it did about the 1890s, we must see the current *Saga* as an expression of where we are today.

THE CAST

Young Jolyon ~ Kenneth More

Soames ~ Eric Porter

Irene ~ Nyree Dawn Porter

Old Jolyon ~ Joseph O'Conor

James ~ John Welsh

Winifred ~ Margaret Tyzack

Ann ~ Fay Compton

Montague ~ Terence Alexander

Bosinney ~ John Bennett

Michael ~ Nicholas Pennell

Swithin ~ George Woodbridge

Fleur ~ Susan Hampshire

Annette ~ Dallia Penn

Jolly ~ Michael York

Jon ~ Martin Jarvis

Hélène ~ Lana Morris

Producer ~ Donald Wilson

BEHIND THE SCENES

DISCOVER HOW THE TEAM CREATED THE NINETEENTH CENTURY FOR THE NEW MILLENNIUM FROM SCRIPTWRITING TO CHOOSING LOCATIONS. MAKING A LAVISH SERIES LIKE *THE FORSYTE SAGA* REQUIRED AN ENORMOUS AMOUNT OF WORK BEHIND THE SCENES, MUCH OF IT TOOK PLACE OVER A YEAR BEFORE THE SERIES HIT OUR SCREENS. HERE ARE THE INDIVIDUAL STORIES OF THE PEOPLE WHO MADE THE SERIES.

THE PRODUCER'S STORY

David Moore at work with Beatrice Batarda who plays Annette.

Nobody undertakes a costume drama lightly. It's an expensive business, at least if you're going to do it right, and it's time-consuming. To commit to a project as large as *The Forsyte Saga* means, basically, signing off the best part of two years of your life.

And it's not just a question of hard work: there's the tricky business of positioning the series in a market that's seen a lot of costume drama over the last few years, where it will be competing for the audience's attention against the ever-growing soaps, against high-profile star vehicles and cheap, easygoing docudramas. In addition to all that, *The Forsyte Saga* brings with it one specific challenge – any new production is instantly going to be compared with the BBC's landmark 1967 series, which set the standards for costume drama over the next twenty years. So, before anyone decided to sign up for *The Forsyte Saga*, they had to be very, very certain of what they were doing.

So why, with all those hurdles to jump, would anyone set about an adaptation of Galsworthy's novels? The simple answer, according to series producer Sita Williams, is that 'they're great books and they've only been adapted once'. The idea came, initially, from David Liddiment, ITV's director of channels, who seized on the Forsyte novels not only as a great achievement in English literature, but also for their iconic status in British TV. The idea was passed on to Williams, a veteran producer at Granada who's equally at home with period drama (*After the War*) and high-profile, contemporary material (Robson Green's *Reckless*). 'My first response was to go and read the books and decide if I felt they were the right thing to adapt in the twenty-first century,' says Williams. 'The first thing that struck me, and that would strike any modern reader picking up *The Man of Property*, is that it's about money, materialism and desire –

which feel like very contemporary subjects. In a way those seem much more the obsessions of this decade than they were of the sixties, when the BBC adaptation was made. We think of the sixties as an idealistic time, whereas our time seems more greedy and competitive.'

Granada were thinking big right from the outset of the project – this was clearly something that couldn't be dashed off as a two-parter. The initial plan was to plan for two series, the first an adaptation of *The Forsyte Saga*, then second moving on to *A*

Modern Comedy. 'There would be no point in boiling these stories down and doing them quickly,' says Williams, 'because the whole point of them is the complexity of the relationships, and the way in which people and families change over time. That requires you to get to know these characters very well, and to see the real detail of their lives. You have to get inside them, to become almost a member of the Forsyte family. That's certainly the experience I had in reading the books. They draw you in. Characters that you don't like at first start to seem like old friends as you learn to understand them. Tiny little insignificant events can take on a greater importance because you see their effect over time. They're big books in every sense of the word – a lot of pages, covering a lot of time, and dealing with big issues – and it would be silly to try to just "tell the story". We had to be ambitious with this or there would have been no point in doing it at all.'

After reading *The Forsyte Saga*, Williams judged that the natural cut-off point for the first series would be the end of *In Chancery*, with the birth of Soames's daughter Fleur.

In action, Chris Menaul prepares Gina McKee and Ioan Gruffudd for a crucial love scene.

'After that there's a big jump forward in time to the 1920s, with a grown-up Fleur and a much older Soames. The BBC did the whole thing right through to *Swan Song*, the end of *A Modern Comedy*, and they just aged the actors up from one week to the next. We didn't want to do that. We decided to tell one chunk of the story at a time, to cast younger actors, take a break, and then leap forward to the 1920s in the next series. I don't like the idea of actors ageing twenty years between one Sunday and the next, and I don't think audiences would accept it so readily now. We're in a very different era of television now. We expect a certain dramatic unity about things. It's better to tell the story in a way that we know will work well on television, that observes the more sophisticated tastes of modern audiences.'

One of the opening scenes, the Forsyte clan gathered together around a lavish dinner table. It took three days to film this one scene at Tabley House near Knutsford.

With this decision made, Williams began to focus on the quality of the material. What sort of books were these? What sort of television would they make? Galsworthy is a transitional writer, pitching his tent somewhere between the established classics of the nineteenth century and the modern masterpieces of Evelyn Waugh, Kingsley Amis and E M Forster. He's not as remote and romantic as Dickens and Austen, but he is distinctly a period piece in a way that those more modern writers are not. *The Forsyte Chronicles* have never quite been accepted in the canon of English classics – and it fast became Williams's goal to establish Galsworthy's ascendancy through a high-quality adaptation of his work.

'It's been said by experts on the subject that bad novels make good television, and *The Forsyte Saga* is often cited as an example. I can understand what people are saying: certain soapy elements that make for second-rate fiction can work extraordinarily well on TV. But I don't think that's fair on Galsworthy. The Forsyte novels are first-rate books. They have their flaws, certainly: *The Man of Property* takes a while to get going, it's overly complex at the start, and the character of Irene is very shakily drawn. But those are minor points that could equally apply to Dickens, whose female characters were far from realistic, or to Thackeray, who was always making mistakes with his plots. Big novels can be unwieldy, it's a fact of life. One point I'm having to make again and again is that *The Forsyte Saga* is a much better book than you might imagine. Galsworthy is out of fashion, but let's not forget that he was one of the most popular writers of his day and he did after all win the Nobel Prize for Literature, mainly because of his achievement with the Forsyte books.

'I think there's a certain amount of snobbery at work here. People think that because the books were made into television that they're slightly less than "real"

literature, that they must be a bit trashy and populist, a bit Barbara Cartland. That is not the case. *The Forsyte Saga* exists first and foremost as fine novels. Any television adaptation, whether it's the BBC's or ours, comes second. The more I thought about it, the more focused I became on the idea that maybe, if nothing else, our adaptation would encourage people to read the books, and then they'd realise how fantastic Galsworthy is. I've started to feel quite evangelical on the subject.'

Williams decided to commit herself to the series at the end of 1999, and by the start of 2000 was talking to writers and working on the adaptation. And, while the scripts were in development (see page 54), another team was being brought together to tackle the logistics of filming such a large piece of television. Six-part series are relatively rare now – commercial pressure has meant that adaptations such as the BBC's *Pride and Prejudice* are less common now than two-parters, such as Granada's own *Nicholas Nickleby*. *The Forsyte Saga*, then, meant calling on the full resources of Granada's production expertise while keeping a strict eye on budgets.

'I was asked to do an appraisal of the project towards the end of 2000,' says the production designer, Stephen Fineren. 'I was given scripts in draft form and a tentative list of locations and set possibilities, and I was asked to work out whether it could be made to work within a certain budget. That meant taking into account everything to do with the physical production: building sets, paying for studio space, props, lighting, the whole lot. Initially we thought of *The Forsyte Saga* as a studio-based series, with all the sets built specially for the show, but it quickly became apparent that this was just not going to work. You'd need a Hollywood-sized budget for that, because a lot of the sets would just not have enough to do. You'd spend a hundred thousand pounds building the dining room at Park Lane and then only use it for two or three scenes. That seemed crazy. So I went back to Granada and suggested that the only way to do this properly was to film the whole thing on location, because at least then you're going into pre-existing places, dressing them as you require, shooting what you need and moving on. It's more complicated from a logistical point of view, because you've got to keep moving everyone around, but it works out a lot cheaper and you get the exact look that you want.'

While Fineren and his team started scouting for locations, Sita Williams was putting together the team that would populate those sets. The first appointment was two directors, Chris Menaul and David Moore, who would take responsibility for three episodes apiece. 'We had to shoot it in two blocks,' says Williams, 'because it would just be too unwieldy as one. The director needs to be involved in the preproduction, then go and actually shoot the thing, and then work on the postproduction, the editing and so on right through to the finished product. It would have taken far too long for one person to handle all of that, so we had to have two directors so that they could work in tandem and bring the show in on time.'

Chris Menaul, who's handling the first three episodes (roughly equivalent to *The Man of Property*), studied the scripts and pondered the visual style that he wanted to

achieve. 'I always use the script as a blueprint. Scripts aren't holy writ for a film: they're there to be interpreted in visual terms. We're shooting this quite differently from other period drama, which tends to be big set pieces and then a lot of talking heads. We're using a lot of long lenses to get close to the action, to foreshorten it, then we're using wide-angle lenses to give a feeling of breadth, or to bring characters looming over the viewer. The opening scene of the first episode should give you a very good idea of what's to come. We're alternating between an intimate scene and a social scene, to set up the parameters of the story to come. You'll see the deserted façade of a house, with the camera zooming in and in until we go through a window and see a child sleeping, with two people standing by the bed and a real frisson between them. That's all done with long lenses, which give a very romantic feel. Then you'll keep cutting away from that to a big dinner-party scene, with fourteen people around the table, all of them filmed very close up with a wide-angle lens, which makes them appear quite overbearing

Sita wanted Damian Lewis as Soames right from the start. 'He has tremendous self-assurance and poise, so you're very drawn to him, but he can also give the impression of being quite distant.'

and formidable. You could have shot that in a traditional way, but it would have looked flat and boring; as it is you've got all these old aunts and grandparents bearing down on you, talking about family and money and breeding, while in the other scene you've got two young people falling in love in long-shot. The visual style establishes the central dichotomy of the story, between love and money, very quickly.'

Of course none of this would be worth a penny without the right actors to bring the original vision to life – and it was the casting process that caused some of the biggest headaches for the creative team. First, there were practical considerations: even within the limited scope of the first two Forsyte novels, the characters would have to age around thirty years from start to finish. Then there were the more intangible criteria – the need to get actors with sufficient gravitas to pull off these difficult roles, but with enough audience appeal to bring the series to life and get good ratings. 'I wasn't worried about going for big TV stars, because the real star of this show is *The Forsyte Saga* itself,' says Sita Williams. 'It's such a famous name that it was always going to grab an audience, more or less whoever we put in it. So my prime concern was in getting really good actors who were right for the part. Any consideration of the kind of profile they might have came afterwards.'

Williams and Menaul began the casting process in February 2001, concentrating on actors in their early thirties for the lead roles of Soames, Irene and Bosinney. 'You can take someone like Damian Lewis, who [was] thirty, and you can easily take him down to his early twenties, which is Soames's age at the start of the story,' says Chris Menaul. 'And it doesn't stretch the credibility too much to take him up to his late forties, which is where we leave him. The BBC adaptation used much older actors, because it was taking them right through to old age, but, looking at it now, it's a bit hard to believe in them with dyed hair and false whiskers when they're playing younger.'

'I had a few people very clearly in my head when we started the casting,' says Sita Williams. 'I was looking for a particular type of actor: not necessarily posh actors, but people who could handle a style that is very different from the social realism that you see in most dramas. Television tends to strive towards the way people really behave in the modern world, and I needed actors who could show how people from the upper classes used to behave around the turn of the century. So they've got to have that seriousness, that emotional restraint – but they've also got to be able to convey to the audience the feelings that are going on under the surface. It's quite a hard trick to pull off.'

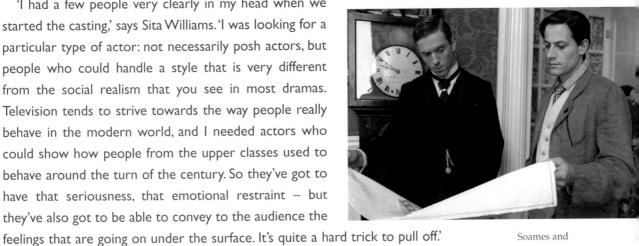

Soames and Bosinney study plans for Robin Hill.

Damian Lewis and Ioan Gruffudd were in the frame right from the start. 'I'd seen them in *Warriors* [Peter Kosminsky's award-winning film about peacekeepers in Bosnia], which I considered to be one of the best films I've seen for a long time,' says Menaul. 'I thought they worked very well together in that, so it's no coincidence that they're both in this.' (Damian Lewis, commenting on the reunion, says 'Gruffudd and Lewis – it sounds like two dodgy solicitors from Swansea.') 'I wanted two young men who were very contrasted in looks and personae, which they are,' says Menaul. 'And they had to be able to bring out all the layers of a character. It would be very easy for some of these characters to come across as one-dimensional, and that would be a disaster, because the whole point of *The Forsyte Saga* is that the more you get to know about people, the more you understand and appreciate them. It would be no good if Soames was just a villain, or if Bosinney was just an arty prig. With Damian and Ioan, you've got two actors who can bring out those depths individually, and who spark off each other very well and add a whole new dimension through that contrast.'

Finding the right
Irene was the
hardest part for
Sita and her team.
'We saw many very
good actresses who
could have played
the role, but Gina
has this quality –
this hauteur – that
makes her right for
Irene.'

Sita Williams had no doubts that Damian Lewis was her Soames. 'Perhaps he's not an obvious choice, but for me he's the only man for the job. From the moment we met him I knew he was it, he was Soames. He has tremendous self-assurance and poise, so you're very drawn to him, but he can also give the impression of being quite distant.' When Lewis was cast in *The Forsyte Saga*, British audiences knew him (if at all) from *Warriors* and from the BBC series *Hearts and Bones*. Since then, of course, he's become internationally famous as the star of Steven Spielberg and Tom Hanks's *Band of Brothers* – a happy coincidence that raises the profile of *The Forsyte Saga* considerably.

'All of that helps, of course,' says Williams, 'but I still wouldn't have cast him if he wasn't right for the job. Damian wasn't sure at first. He said to me, "But surely you don't want a red-haired Soames, do you?" The colour of his hair just doesn't matter! What I like is this chilly, interior quality that he has, combined with the fact that a lot of people find him tremendously attractive. That's the key. You have to see him being cruel and unsympathetic towards Irene, but you have to be sufficiently attracted to him to want to dig a bit deeper and understand why he's behaving this way. Most actors just want to be loved in whatever role they play, but Damian's always been very keen to bring out the cruelty in Soames as well as the more admirable qualities. That way you can see him doing wrong, but you can also understand that he's the architect of his own destruction. I've watched some of the rushes and I've sat there going, "Oh, no, Soames, please don't do that!" I hope that audiences will be shouting at their televisions in exactly the same way. You can see why Irene hates him, but he just can't stop himself. He never says what he really wants to say, he gets it all wrong and he ends up doing terrible things within that relationship.'

The role of Bosinney is much less complex. 'You have to be careful that he doesn't come across as an arrogant prat,' says Williams, 'and that will never happen because Ioan Gruffudd is just the most fall-in-loveable-with young actor around. I defy anybody not to find him attractive. He's very upbeat, and his Welsh accent comes through, which makes him seem warm and passionate, a total contrast to Soames. Bosinney has extraordinary self-belief, which can look like arrogance, but it's tempered by this real warmth. You can see immediately why Irene falls in love with him. He's everything she's longed for and has never had.'

The hardest piece of casting was the search for the right Irene. She's an elusive character – even Galsworthy admitted that he'd drawn her in shadows, that she presented a different façade to every character in the book and to every reader. Williams and Menaul saw an awful lot of actresses before they settled on Gina McKee. 'We were looking for someone with a real sense of mystique,' says Menaul. 'Obviously

Wendy Craig as
Aunt Juley during
the painstaking
filming of the
dinner party in
episode one.

we wanted someone beautiful and sexy, because it's Irene's physical attractiveness as much as anything that disrupts the Forsyte family, but she had to be mysterious as well. Part of the appeal of Irene is that you want to unwrap the enigma. Gina has a natural elegance, what I would call a period look – the sort of style that you see in paintings from the turn of the century, somewhat aloof and untouchable. We saw many very good actresses who could have played the role, but Gina has this quality – this hauteur – that makes her right for Irene.'

Williams, once again, was looking for an actress who could convey the right blend of light and shade. 'I didn't want Irene to be nothing more than a victim. You have to engage with her, to see her faults as well as her virtues. To some extent, I want to grab Irene by the shoulders and shake her, to say, "Oh, come on, woman! Pull yourself together! He's not *that* bad – just make the most of your life and stop complaining!" So there's that side of her which is quite unsympathetic, but then there's the inner woman who is desperate for love and who feels that she's been sold into marriage. None of the characters in *The Forsyte Saga* are entirely good or entirely bad. It's never black or white. *The Forsyte Saga* really is a composition in various shades of grey, like a Whistler painting.'

With the three leads in place, Williams and Menaul then had the enviable experience of watching the cream of the British acting profession flocking to their production. *The Forsyte Saga* boasts more recognisable faces than any drama in recent memory – a testament, says Williams, to the status of the property. 'The Forsyte Saga* is regarded as a landmark show for all sorts of reasons,' she says. 'Obviously a lot of people still remember the 1967 adaptation, which became one of the most famous programmes of all time; we actually had one actress coming along to audition with a double-page spread from the *Daily Mail* that her mother had saved and dug out for her. There's a huge brand awareness involved, so we knew that agents would want to get their clients into the show. It has an inbuilt prominence that is really none of our doing. But I'd also like to be immodest and say that the scripts are great, and that attracted a lot of people. We couldn't just say to people "Come and be in our show" if we didn't have some really good material to attract them with.

'I'm also very keen to stress that this is not in any sense a "remake" of an existing television programme. People keep saying, "Granada are remaking *The Forsyte Saga*", but that's a complete misunderstanding of what it is. *The Forsyte Saga* is a set of books, not a TV series. We're not attempting to "remake" what the BBC did. I watched a couple of episodes just to get an idea of how they'd set about it, but I didn't go any further than that because I did not want our production to be influenced by anybody else's work. We've gone back to the source, to Galsworthy, and we're adapting that. Nobody ever says, "Oh, they're remaking that 1970s version of *Oliver Twist* or that 1980s version of *Bleak House*" – they understand that it's a reinterpretation of the book, in the same way that each new production of a Shakespeare play is a reinterpretation of the text. What we're doing is reinterpreting Galsworthy for our times, because we believe that the books are important and have a lot to say to us.'

The Forsyte Saga has been filmed almost entirely on location in the northwest of England, within a fifty-mile radius of Granada's Manchester base. This is for two reasons. First, with a large cast and dozens of locations, it was desirable to avoid traipsing the length and breadth of the country for each new setup. Secondly, the northwest offered the producers just the right blend of locations to recreate the action of *The Forsyte*

Saga, which, of course, never strays too far from London and its satellites.

'We did think at one time of filming it in London,' says Sita Williams, 'but we needed largely Georgian architecture, and London just doesn't give you Georgian London any more. The few remaining bits of Georgian architecture are in areas so crowded that it would be impossible to film there. Fortunately, Liverpool does give you street after street of Georgian architecture, and the northwest gives you exactly the kind of houses that the Forsytes would have lived in.'

One such is Tabley House, an extravagantly beautiful house set in vast grounds near Knutsford. It's one of those places where, with very little imagination, one can forget all about the twenty-first century. Green parkland rolls away as far as the eye can see, the traffic noise is muted and distant, the only sound to disturb the ear is the caw of rooks or the bleat of sheep. The travelling *Forsyte Saga* circus reached Tabley in August 2001, about a third of the way into the filming – the house provided just the right sort of interior for Park Lane, the home of James and Emily Forsyte, and with very little in the way of extra dressing could furnish a dinner party for a dozen or so guests. For that crucial first scene in Episode One, when Dartie is introduced as Winifred's fiancé, the entire clan gather to chew their way through a large piece of mutton and to assess the fortunes of this new addition to the family.

It's a painstaking piece of filming; the room has been dressed with a bit of Chinese pottery and a few extra pictures, but the real work goes into the meticulous setting up of every single shot. This is a complex scene: the camera travels from one face to the next, each of them filmed in wide-angle so that they seem to burst out of the screen, completely dominating the tender, romantic scene with which this will eventually be spliced. And it's not enough for each actor to come in, do his or her turn and then go back to the trailer for a nap: everyone has to be there for every shot, providing the background chatter, the atmosphere, against which the featured characters will be presented. The dining table, fully dressed for an establishing shot with linen and silverware, has been removed to allow the cameras full access to the actors, who nevertheless have to carry on lifting forkfuls of food to their mouths. As the camera moves round the table, the 'off-duty' actors can relax to a certain degree: wigs are removed, ties undone, shoes replaced with flip-flops or trainers. Thus, while the spot-light's on Wendy Craig as fluttery Aunt Juley, making indiscreet remarks about Jolyon's governess, Damian Lewis can sit opposite her in jeans and a T-shirt, saying Soames's lines but looking like anything but a Forsyte.

While the hard work goes on in the dining room, the supporting artists and off-duty actors relax in adjacent rooms, with wardrobe and make-up artists fussing over the

Bosinney and June:
a complete contrast
to Soames and
Irene.

Filming a major TV drama can be hard work!

final details before they're allowed on set. Newspapers are spread over marble-topped tables; mobile phones are whipped out as soon as the director has yelled 'Cut!' Damian Lewis, when he's not needed for a shot, nips off to a little antechamber he's found further along the wing, where he can practise the piano.

In the dining room, all is atmospheric gloom as the dinner party grinds on. Outside, the sun is shining brilliantly through one of those light mists that glare the eye. Anyone who's not needed for the next hour or so is trying to find a spot where they can sunbathe without undoing the meticulous work of the dressers; it's absolutely forbidden to sit on damp grass. At the unit base – a collection of trucks and trailers about three hundred yards from the main house – Ioan Gruffudd and Gillian Kearney are having their photograph taken in full costume, with the rolling fields behind them. The photographer is framing the shot with great care – the grass all around their neatly shod feet is littered with cowpats. This is meant to be Hyde Park, let us not forget, and even in the 1880s cows did not graze in central London. For an extra-modern touch, the gateway between the car park and the fields is carpeted all around with foam matting drenched with a particularly pungent disinfectant – here in Cheshire, foot-and-mouth is still a concern.

So, for now, the *Forsyte Saga* circus has completed its six-month tour of the stately homes of the northwest. Granada has deployed its considerable resources to bring Galsworthy's books to life – not just the stories and the characters, but the details that make up the fabric of the Forsytes' lives, so important to Galsworthy and to generations of readers since. 'It pained me when the press got the wrong end of the stick and started saying that we were doing the entire Forsyte Saga in six episodes, as opposed to the 26 that the BBC did,' says Sita Williams. 'It gave the impression that we were skimping on it, just doing a quickie adaptation, which couldn't have been further from the truth. The BBC adaptation covered an awful lot more ground than us: they went right up to the end of *Swan Song*, the sixth novel, whereas we're just doing the first two books. I think on an hour-by-hour basis, we're almost the same.'

And this, of course, begs a question: what of the future? 'The will is there to do more,' says Williams. 'Obviously, as soon as you take on something like *The Forsyte Saga*, you're faced with exactly the same issues that faced Galsworthy: you've started these characters on a journey, and you want to take them as far as possible. When we made the decision just to film the first two books for this first six-part series, we knew that we would like to carry on and tackle the next block of books. It isn't absolutely commissioned at this stage – obviously a lot depends on how the first series is received. But we're already in the planning stages, mapping out where we might start a second series, how far we could take it, what we should concentrate on to tell the story well and to be faithful to Galsworthy's intentions. All the actors are contracted for a second series, and we're already outlining it. Now we just have to wait and see.'

As *Forsyte* readers will know, the stories just keep getting better and better, and the drama surrounding Soames's daughter Fleur and her unsatisfactory marriage is one of the highlights of the *Chronicles*. Soames is still there, an observer more than a protagonist, while the presence of Irene hovers over the characters like a ghost. And there's the final, ironic working out of the Jolyon saga …

But for all this we shall simply have to watch and wait.

Cast and crew queuing in a very unForsytian way for their lunch.

THE WRITERS' STORIES

Adapting a famous novel for television is like a tightrope act. Veer too much towards the conventions of contemporary TV drama, and you'll have the book's fans shouting 'betrayal!' and 'travesty!' from the sidelines. Treat the source material with too much reverence, and you risk creating dull, overly cautious drama that won't grab the attention of modern audiences. The best adaptations of the last ten years have been clever sleights-of-hand, taking liberties here and there, changing where necessary but doing it in such a deft, elegant way that no one is any the wiser. But, for all the good adaptations, there are usually a couple of duffs along the way – just in case anyone thought that this was an easy way of making drama.

Damian Lewis quickly brushes up on his lines before filming begins.

Sita Williams was determined that her production of *The Forsyte Saga* should reach the biggest audience possible while remaining true to the spirit of the books. 'I wanted writers who would understand exactly what Galsworthy is all about, who could enter into the spirit of *The Forsyte Saga*, but who could also provide us with some very sharp scripts.' She turned first to Stephen Malatrat, with whom she'd worked on *The Innocent*, and sent him a copy of Galsworthy. 'He got it immediately – he understood Galsworthy's irony, his radicalism, his feminism. The first thing he said to me is, "Oh, he's sending up *The Man of Property*, he's having fun with him." And that's exactly right. Galsworthy adores his central character, but he's a very flawed hero. That's quite unusual for a novel of this period – the hero is a seriously flawed character. That's very modern, I think. People are flawed. None of us is a storybook hero.'

Clearly this was a job for more than one writer – with the schedules that Granada had in mind, nobody was going to have the leisure to set about adapting both *The Man of Property* and *In Chancery* in one go. So Williams recruited another writer, someone she felt would provide a sympathetic balance to Malatrat. 'Stephen's old enough to remember *The Forsyte Saga* when it was first on television, so I wanted someone younger to whom it would mean nothing at all,' says Williams. 'I chose Jan McVerry because, first and foremost, she's a woman, and I think it's important to bring out the female aspects of Galsworthy's writing, and secondly because she was born after 1967 and had never seen the BBC adaptation.'

Malatrat and McVerry had worked together before on another large-scale continuing Granada drama – none other than *Coronation Street*, for which he was a scriptwriter and she a storyliner in the early nineties. 'Then I went on to become a scriptwriter as well,' says McVerry. 'Granada liked the idea that both Stephen and I had a soap back-ground – they thought we'd understand the value of big, bold stories. The Forsyte novels are full of that, and in some ways they're like highbrow soap opera. There are cliffhangers, lots of coincidences, overlapping stories, the sort of stuff that we're very used to as TV writers. Galsworthy's very witty, too, and I think you need writers who will bring out the humour – there's a danger that it could be very po-faced. Stephen and I comple-ment each other well: he's much more considered, thoughtful and laid back, whereas I'm gobby and impulsive. Between us we make up a sort of composite Galsworthy.'

McVerry's first task was to get reading. 'My first instinct was to say no to this job. As soon as I looked at the books I realised that it was going to be an enormous commitment, and as I've got two very young children the time just didn't seem right. Sita Williams had to do a certain amount of arm-twisting. Once I read the novels, though, I became quite eager to get cracking. I expected it to be quite dry and stiff, in an *Upstairs, Downstairs* kind of way. I thought Galsworthy would be very much on the side of the upper-class characters. But it's a big surprise: he's very funny, very sharp, and he has a definite political leaning towards socialism and feminism. He's not writing about perfect, ideal English people. He had an agenda, and he works it through his characters.'

Writers and producer sat down together in February 2000 to work out what exactly they were going to show on screen. There are certain fundamental problems with the

'Soames is a fascinating character for any writer to play with because he's so complex' says writer Jan McVerry.

narrative structure: Galsworthy introduces a lot of material in the form of flashbacks, which would clearly have to be shown if TV audiences were to make head or tail of it. 'The novels actually start with the engagement of June to Bosinney,' says Sita Williams, 'right in the middle of the story. You learn about Soames's wooing of Irene, and about Young Jolyon's affair with the governess, Helene, through the gossip and memories of the other characters. It's great for a novel, but not for TV. This isn't like adapting Dickens, who wrote perfect, straightforward, linear narratives. Galsworthy is much more involved than that. So we had to look at the back story and tease out the important things and put them on screen.'

It was easy for the writers to get carried away by the comic aspects of the book, particularly with Dartie (below) . . .

Thus the first ninety-minute episode contains all the background to the starting point of the novels, with the introduction of Bosinney to the family circle. 'I fought hard for long episodes,' says Williams. 'You need time and space to introduce the characters and to go into the details. We took three days to film the single dinner party that kicks off Episode One, but by the time you've seen that you really know these people.'

There were other tough decisions to be made: Galsworthy's novels contain dozens of secondary characters and sub-plots that would simply clog up a TV adaptation. 'We're concentrating on the strongest stories,' says Jan McVerry. 'We went through the novels and decided which episodes were going into the script and which weren't. You have to do that with any adaptation: you can't represent every incidental character or you'd go on for thousands of hours and bore everyone to death. This is drama, and you have to pare it down a bit. On the other hand, there are some holes in the narrative that we wanted to fill in. The death of Bosinney, for instance, happens out of sight in the novel, but it's such a dramatic highlight that we felt we had to show it. We thought long and hard about it, and I think we started off being a little over-respectful to the novels – you could end up with something not very dramatic, and that would do nobody any favours.'

The writing process took the best part of a year, with Malatrat and McVerry in a constant process of consultation with producer and directors, until everyone was satisfied that the best possible drama had been squeezed out of Galsworthy's novels. 'Television writers don't write alone,' says Williams. 'It's a very collaborative process, because a lot of other people are going to be involved in getting this to the screen. I worked with them constantly on structure and narrative, worrying away at certain points like whether or not we were bringing Irene to life, whether we were maintaining a balance of sympathy with Soames. I started off looking at some of the BBC adaptation, because of course I was curious to see how they'd done it, but I had to stop very quickly. There's was a very different approach. They used material from some of the short stories, they went into some of the digressions about the minor characters, which you just couldn't do now. I've always insisted that our source for this production is Galsworthy, not the BBC adaptation, and anyone who looks at them side by side will see a complete difference in approach.'

'It's so hard,' says McVerry, 'because you have to keep going back to the novels to make sure you're being faithful to the story, and observing the conventions

. . .and Aunt Juley, two of the great clowns of the story.

of how people expressed their emotions. You can't just create a character and make them say what they feel. These people are not like that. They talk around subjects, they're not spontaneous. It's very different from writing contemporary, original TV drama. I've also been working on *Clocking Off*, and that's so different – it's much freer and easier than this, because you're in charge of the characters, and your only responsibility is to yourself. Adapting is a very specialised skill, and not something that any writer can take on lightly.'

That said, McVerry has been bitten hard by the Galsworthy bug. 'Soames is absolutely fascinating for any writer to play with, because he's so complex. There's a temptation to rein him back a bit and make him more sympathetic, because for all his faults you do end up loving him. But the producer was always pushing us to go further, to bring out his dark side, and I was worried that people would just hate him. Now I've seen Damian Lewis's performance, though, I'm not worried, because he brings out all the sympathetic sides of the character that the words themselves don't always contain. Soames is a very disturbed individual, and it's interesting for a woman to write for him. I mean, he's a rapist! But you can understand what's driven him to it. You can see the turmoil in his mind that's twisted him into doing a thing like that.

'Irene is very different. She's a modern woman, she flouts convention. I think she comes into focus when you see her in the flesh. She's a blank in the books. Like a lot of male writers, Galsworthy holds up this stereotype of a woman who's both the Madonna and the whore. She's very sketchy: she can be cold and calculating one minute, warm and sexy the next. We've tried to flesh her out a bit, to see how she gets between those two extremes. June says to Irene at one point, "You have the sweetest voice, and yet you say the cruellest things" – and that's the essence of Irene. It would be easy to make her a heroine, but she's not perfect.'

It was the minor characters who caused McVerry the biggest problems, though. 'I loved writing for the family members. They're so silly, and they're such fun to write for. There's an awful lot of comic material in the books, so it's easy to get carried away. We had to conflate a few of the characters – we've concentrated, really, on Aunt Juley and Aunt Hester, and they're a great double act. I ended up writing pages of comic dialogue for them, and for Dartie, who is the other great clown in the books. They're so sparky and funny, but sadly they don't do a great deal to advance the plot. Sita had to keep telling me to pull back on the family stuff, which was very hard. It's like killing your own babies. Galsworthy's novels give us such a huge, rich tapestry that you want to represent every single stitch. It would be lovely to write, but unfortunately it wouldn't be drama.'

THE DESIGNERS' STORIES

SET DESIGN

Once upon a time, television producers were content to create their shows in the studio, with rickety walls and wobbly furniture that wouldn't have looked out of place in an impoverished regional rep. Now, however, as TV drama has grown up and production values have soared, the search is on for ever-greater authenticity. Since the BBC's 1995 adaptation of *Pride and Prejudice*, sets and locations have become the stars of TV drama almost as much as the actors themselves.

So, when Granada set about making *The Forsyte Saga*, the production team knew that they would have to find sets that would give the impression of lavish opulence – not to mention accurate period detail – within the budget and within a practical distance from the Manchester HQ. 'I did my first recce in London,' says the production designer, Stephen Fineren. 'I went to the actual locations that are mentioned in the books – Green Street, Montpelier Square, Hyde Park and so on – and took a lot of photographs of the buildings that are still there. Then I went north and tried to find things that matched!'

London was never seriously considered as a location: besides the inconvenience of dragging the entire cast and crew all the way down the M6, there is simply not enough

The Bower exterior, Gambier Terrace in Liverpool. The entrance door does not exist so a false porch wall was built between the pillars where the actors could 'hide' instead of going through the door.

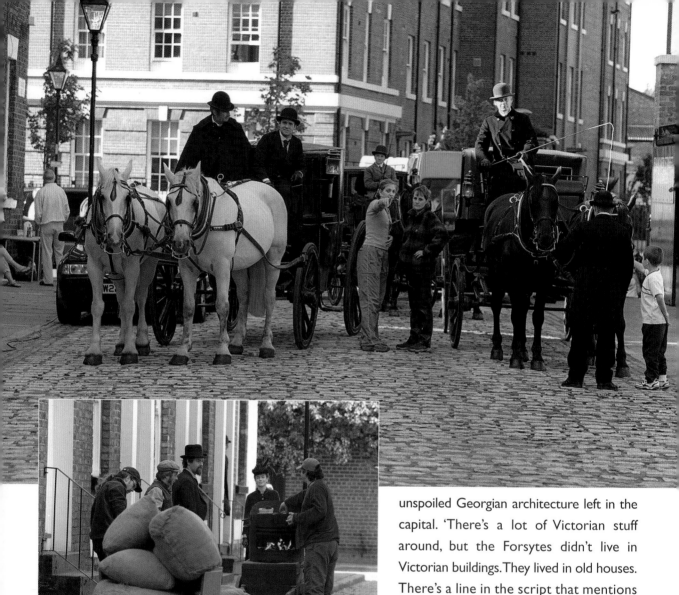

unspoiled Georgian architecture left in the capital. 'There's a lot of Victorian stuff around, but the Forsytes didn't live in Victorian buildings. They lived in old houses. There's a line in the script that mentions the fact that Soames is the first Forsyte for a generation actually to build a house; I think they felt much more at home in the buildings of an earlier generation.' Fortunately, the northwest of England is

Creating a Victorian street scene. Main picture, two coaches stand ready for action and (inset) setting up a brazier.

rich in Georgian streets and houses, 'and there's not a single building in the area that we didn't consider,' says Fineren. 'We visited a colossal number of locations before we found what we wanted. Basically we found that Liverpool offered us the best choice. Manchester is too Victorian, whereas Liverpool has a lot of fabulous Georgian streets. The only problem is that they're pretty run down; the Georgian survivals tend to be in rather depressed areas, so they need a fair bit of work to bring them up to scratch. But by Christmas 2000 I'd found locations to match everything in the script, and I presented it all to the producers in a document, then went off to do a film in Ireland.'

By the time Fineren returned, production on *The Forsyte Saga* had cranked up a notch or two. 'Suddenly we had to turn these ideas into reality,' says Fineren. 'I started working with Chris Menaul, the director of the first three episodes, and making final decisions on what would actually work on screen. Chris rejected a

The contrast between Mrs Heron's overstuffed sitting room and the sumptuous interiors of the more wealthy Forsyte family is very apparent.

lot of the locations as being simply not grand enough. You have to remember that the houses that families like the Forsytes were living in, around Hyde Park, for instance, were enormous – they were real country houses in the heart of London. So we had to find existing country houses, like Croxteth Hall and Lyme Hall, that provided façades of sufficient grandeur for a posh mansion in town. After that it was just a question of dressing them properly.'

This sounds a lot simpler than it really is. 'Dressing' an exterior means not only putting in a few net curtains and changing the door knockers: all evidence of the twentieth and twenty-first centuries has to be eradicated, or at least obscured. 'At Croxteth Hall, which we used for James and Emily's house in Park Lane, we had to strip out all the electric wires on the front of the house and then have the whole thing repainted. It was in a dilapidated state, and scheduled for repainting in any case, so I think we did them a favour. We made it nice and clean and white, then we had to net all the windows with lacy curtains, and build railings and gates on the exterior. There was a tarmac area in front with a rough bit of parkland beyond it, so we covered the tarmac with crushed gravel to simulate the old surface of Park Lane, and built a fence through which you could glimpse Hyde Park. Obviously you can't completely rebuild everything, so you have to use scenic elements in a suggestive way. A couple of strategically placed urns can save an awful lot, and save a good deal of money.'

Such cost-cutting measures were not always possible. At Faulkener Square in Liverpool, which stands in for Montpelier Square, home of Soames and Irene, there was some serious restoration to be done. 'A lot of my budget went on doing up Faulkener Square,' says Fineren. 'We had to change all the doors in a run of fifty houses. A lot of

(above) Winifred and Dartie's Green Street drawing room, smaller and more cramped than James and Emily's.

(centre) Tabley House provided the setting for James and Emily's Park Lane drawing room.

the buildings round there are used as student accommodation, and they're a bit run down. We put new front doors, fanlights and net curtains on the whole lot, which was a hard day's work. Then, once you've got the houses up to scratch, you have to start hiding the things you can't move. We built a lot of fences to cover things up; we placed a good deal of vegetation around the square; and I developed a sort of universal work-man's hut for covering up cars. It straddles the pavement and half the road. You can dress it up with braziers and ladders and it obscures everything behind it, including rows of parked cars. It's modelled on something I saw in an old photograph of a London bridge, and it got me out of a lot of trouble.'

Once the sets were dressed and ready, Fineren had to fill them with mobile scenery to give the impression of a busy Victorian street. 'My rule is to put in as much activity as I can afford. This was a medium-budget show, so we could afford a fair amount. Outside Croxteth we had seven carriages, which was about as big as it got. I've worked on much bigger-budget TV programmes, like *Sherlock Holmes*, where we'd stick a dozen horses and carriages in one tiny street, and then add a few extra street vendors for good measure. On *The Forsyte Saga* we had to draw in a bit from that kind of extravagance, but I don't think you'll notice the difference.'

One factor, however, was beyond Fineren's control: much of *The Forsyte Saga* was filmed while foot-and-mouth restrictions applied. 'In Lyme Park there were fences everywhere to keep the deer back, and we weren't allowed to bring any horses in. So

Old Jolyon's book-
lined study is very
characteristic of
the man.

we said OK, we'll just haul the carriages in and they'll be parked up, you won't see the horses. By the time the restrictions were lifted, we were so far into the filming that we didn't have any budget left for horses.'

With the exteriors in the bag, Fineren turned his attention to interiors. Studio sets had already been rejected as too expensive – and so appropriate rooms had to be found in existing locations. 'It's a question of scale, initially. You have to find rooms that convey the size of a house. Park Lane, where James and Emily live, is a huge house, whereas Montpelier Square, Soames's home, is a more conventional town house. Green Street, where Winifred and Dartie live, is much smaller and less grand. It's practically impossible to find all the right rooms for one house in the same building, so we were scattered all over the place. For instance, if you look at the Park Lane locations – we filmed the exteriors at Croxteth Hall, then the bedroom was at Arley, the drawing room at Lyme Park, the reception room and the dining room at Tabley House. It's a completely schizophrenic way of working, and you just have to make sure that each of these scattered rooms is dressed in a way that will make sense when they're all brought together on screen. They have to work as part of the same imaginary house, even though they're miles apart in reality.'

Fineren's team concentrated on furniture and fabrics, aiming for a unity of style, taste and colour. 'Tabley House was more or less perfect when we went in. It has beautiful red and gold flock wallpaper, and a great collection of paintings from the right period.

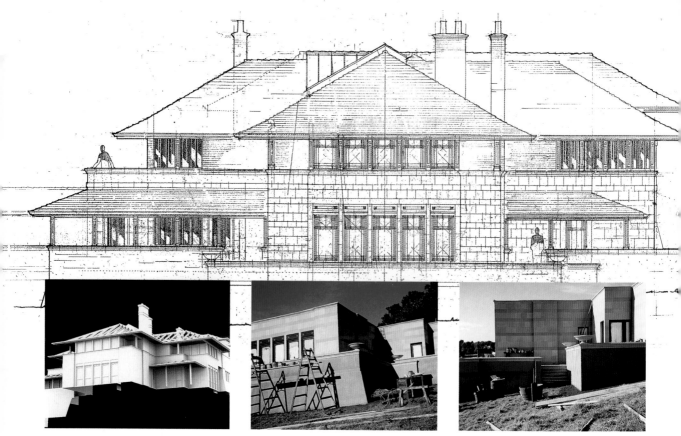

Inspired by the architects Frank Lloyd Wright and Edward Godwin, only the first floor of Robin Hill was actually built, the second story was computer-generated.

All we had to do was put in a bit of furniture that we hired from London, and scatter a few props. The furniture was trundling up and down the motorway in huge lorries. It's like moving house about thirty times in a year.'

The northwest is particularly blessed with Georgian architecture, which mopped up 90 per cent of the location requirements. One building, however, stood out like a sore thumb the moment that Fineren read the scripts. 'Soames has a brand-new house built at Robin Hill. Again and again we're told how modern and unusual it is, and it becomes almost a character in the story. I knew straightaway that we were going to have to build this one.'

Robin Hill is commissioned by Soames from Phil Bosinney, the unconventional young architect who's engaged to June, as a country retreat that he hopes will save his unhappy marriage to Irene. Bosinney is ahead of his time – not Art Nouveau, certainly not classical, and beyond arts and crafts. 'There are only three real arts-and-crafts exteriors in the North of England, but even they didn't look strong enough, different enough, for Robin Hill. I showed photographs to Chris Menaul, and he said we'd just have to build half the set and digitise the rest.'

Fineren found inspiration for his creation in the works of four designers: the American Frank Lloyd Wright, the Scottish Charles Rennie Mackintosh, and the English

Charles Voysey and Edward Godwin. 'I saw an early sketch by Wright which was absolutely stunning: all foreshortened sightlines, rectilinear shapes, horizontal planes rather than the solid bulk so beloved of the Victorians. So I thought, well, if Frank Lloyd Wright could do that in 1890, then Philip Bosinney can do it in 1883. I've cheated by seven years, but my excuse is that Bosinney is just way, way ahead of his time. Chris [Menaul] and Sita [Williams, the producer] loved it, and so we had our blueprint for the overall feel. But Wright was really too extreme: I had to introduce other more traditional

layers, otherwise it just wouldn't be believable as a house that Soames Forsyte would commission, however good his taste. That's where I turned to Godwin, who's one of my favourite architects. He was greatly influenced by Japanese stuff, he loved simple lines, black wood, a very clean look. He designed a house in 1865 that was so advanced it never got planning permission. He was very much part of the Aesthetic movement at the end of the century, and I think that's the sort of person that Bosinney would have been. Rather unconventional in his ideas and his looks, and certainly in his love life.'

Voysey and Mackintosh provided inspiration for the decoration of Robin Hill — simple stonework panels, stained glass, furniture design. 'Anyone who's studied architecture or decorative arts will see elements of all these designers and a few more,' says Fineren, 'but I hope the whole thing works together as a unit. I tried to some extent to be faithful to Galsworthy's descriptions of Robin Hill in the books, but actually they're not at all practical. There are too many columns crammed into the inner courtyard — he talks about eight, and I've cut it down to four, otherwise it would have been too crowded. I've stuck to the key things — there are no interior doors, for instance, which some of the characters find a bit shocking, and was something that Wright liked to do. He just put curtains across interior doorways. The main feature of the interior is the flowing space, which is something Galsworthy talks about. You can see from one room into the next,

Charles Rennie Mackintosh and Charles Voysey were the inspiration for the interior of Robin Hill – simple stonework panels, stained glass and furniture design. The result is a beautiful, light and spacious interior which looks remarkably modern.

Stephen Fineran tried to be faithful to Galsworthy's description of Robin Hill, for example there are no interior doors, and you can easily see from one room into the next.

(right) Main picture shows John Singer Sargent's famous 'Madame X'. (right inset) James Tissot's 'Mrs Newton with a parasol'. Both artists provided inspiration for Phoebe de Gaye as she set about designing the costumes.

your eye can rest on objects very far away, which provides a big contrast to the other interiors, where all the space is divided up into little boxes and there's a rather claustrophobic feel. Robin Hill is all to do with freedom – freedom from London, freedom from convention – and that's expressed through the sense of light and space that you get nowhere else in the story.'

What you'll see on screen is a mixture of the real and the virtual. The ground floor and garden terrace of Robin Hill was built on a hillside in Cheshire; everything else is computer-generated. 'We built as much as we possibly could; it's about fourteen feet high all the way around so that the actors could walk freely without going out of frame, as it were. The rest of it is done in postproduction, so we could show the house in various stages of completion. You see it as a building site, you see it as a finished house with a family living in it, and there was no way that we could ever have afforded to build that. We went wildly over budget as it is.'

COSTUME DESIGN

While the set-design team scoured the country for the right settings for *The Forsyte Saga*, the wardrobe and make-up artists were concentrating on the human element. Unlike many other costume dramas, which either take place in a very short period of time (*Pride and Prejudice*) or tend towards nonspecific, fantastical elements (*Oliver Twist*), *The Forsyte Saga* takes place over several decades and has its roots firmly in historical reality. We know a good deal about how people dressed, talked and acted around the turn of the century; it's a period that still has an immediacy for us, if it's not quite within living memory. So the Forsyte look had to be accurate, and had to express something very subtle about the English class system and its social niceties.

The costume designer, Phoebe De Gaye, aimed for historical accuracy, but concedes that 'any interpretation of the past says a good deal about the time in which it's made. If you look at the costumes for the 1967 version of *The Forsyte Saga*, they look incredibly sixties to us! It's a mixture of high Victorian and pure sixties, right down to the eye make-up and the decorations on the dresses. I'm sure people will look back on this one day and say, "Oh God, it's so 2002!" That's not a bad thing. We're not creating a museum exhibit. I hope that we're saying something about the time in which we live, and our relationship with the past.'

De Gaye started the job by searching for paintings from the period that had the right 'flavour' for what she had in mind. 'I wanted this to be an attractive programme; we're dealing with people from a certain level of society who could afford nice things, and who, as far as we know, spent a good deal of money on their houses and their personal appearance. They're not showy people, but there's a lot of restrained opulence in what they wear. They express their social status as much through their clothes as through their houses or their words. Also, this is, to some extent, a love story – it's about how people judge each other, what they find attractive in each other – and I wanted to get that across in the clothes.'

Initial inspiration came from the decorative paintings

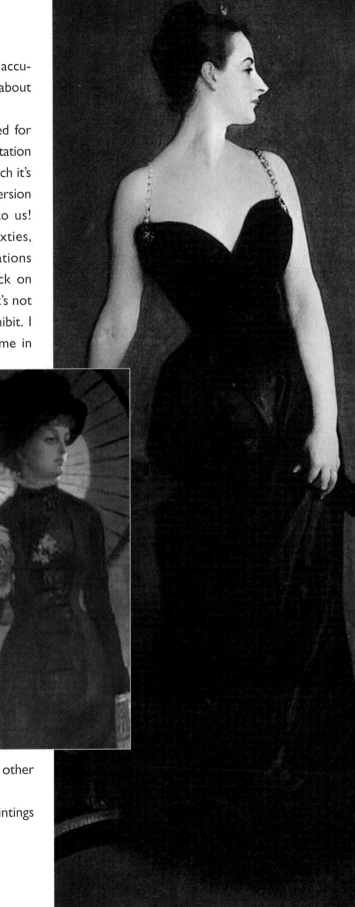

of Whistler, Tissot and Sargent, who provided De Gaye with a pallet of colours and an idea of fabric textures. 'Fabrics at that time, particularly those used for women's dresses, came in the most incredible textures and lustres. They used a lot of velvet, feathers and lace, silk, satin, taffeta, all those wonderful materials that are a joy to work with. Within that basic format, though, there is a great deal of variation. The older women in the cast, the aunts and that generation, hark back to a high Victorian feel, groaning under acres of trim and lace. They went for a very feminine look with lots of little grace notes, and ended up basically looking overupholstered. Then at the opposite extreme there's the character of Irene, who looks forward to the more modern woman.'

This was the era of dress reform, when a number of women – and several sympathetic men – strove to free the female wardrobe from the restrictions of the corset and the bustle, those strange sartorial inventions that rendered many women short of breath and basically unable to move without assistance. 'Irene is a transitional figure,' says De Gaye. 'Her style is markedly more modern – she wears strong colours and cleaner shapes, she doesn't go in for

Irene's beautiful red ball gown was partly inspired by John Singer Sargent's 'Madame X'.

much trim – but she's not quite there. She's not freed herself from the conventions of her time. I would have loved to dress Gina McKee in some really modern-looking clothes but it would have been wrong for the character. Mind you, she looks great in anything I put on her, and she's incredibly patient with all the fittings that were required. She was quite content to stand around for hours in a corset while I fussed with a piece of velvet, so I have to say that she was a joy to dress.'

The men's wardrobe is, by and large, a conservative affair, the Forsytes being a conservative family at a time of rigid formality in dress. 'Soames is dressed soberly and strictly throughout the entire series, always in black and grey, always looking as if he's going to a funeral even when he's at a party. Lounge suits were starting to come in for men in the 1890s, but Soames sticks to frock coats – he's old-fashioned in his dress even when he's a relatively young man. That says a lot about his character, especially when you contrast him to the character of Bosinney, who is basically a man of the twentieth century. Bosinney wears looser, soft-collared shirts, coloured linen and soft hats, which the Forsytes find absolutely shocking. It's a romantic, dashing look that I based very loosely on Lord Alfred Douglas [Oscar Wilde's lover], who wore some really extraordinary clothes for his time. Bosinney is an aesthete, and a free spirit, a threat to the Forsyte way of life, and even his clothes are a challenge to them. Both Damian [Lewis, as Soames] and Ioan [Gruffudd, as Bosinney] are complete clothes horses, and they look gorgeous in the wardrobe we've put together for them. Ioan in particular is a complete poser and he loved swanning around in all these flowing coats and colourful ties.'

As well as designing for the principle characters, De Gaye is also responsible for dressing the crowds of supporting artists. 'I went through every script and took a note of all the different environments we found ourselves in. These ranged from high-society balls to casinos to streets full of prostitutes. Then I immersed myself in the period, finding as much visual reference as I could, copying hundreds of pictures and sorting them into piles for different social groups. It's a huge jigsaw puzzle that you have to tweak all the time, because once you've got the main characters cast and dressed you have to adjust the crowd scenes to create the right contrast. It's a very collaborative process – I'm always talking to the director and to the make-up team, and gradually we all agree on a look and we go with it.'

Most of the costumes for *The Forsyte Saga* came

Soames is old fashioned in his dress and sticks to frock coats throughout the series.

Phoebe's sketches for two of Irene's dresses. Left: a dishevelled look after she has made love with Bosinney. Right: A much more demure dress for the supper with Soames, June and Bosinney. Below: Barbara Flynn trying on one of Emily Forsyte's sumptuous gowns.

IRENE
after making love on Robin Hill

fabulous tangled mass of silk and underwear

IRENE
stilted supper with Bosinney & June

creamy lace

onebred velvet corset echoed in fan to at neck worn on

soft opening

green taffeta

sharp sweep fan to

from the big hire houses in London, where existing pieces could be trimmed, resized or made over by one of De Gaye's team of assistants. Completely new costumes were designed by De Gaye according to the dictates of the script and the fabrics available. 'I sat in my office surrounded by samples of material, sketching and taking notes and referring to measurements. It's all done now, give or take the odd prostitute.'

An unexpected review of De Gaye's handiwork came from a nine-year-old boy in Liverpool, who was watching Amanda Root [Winifred] walking to the location in Princes Park. 'She was rigged up in one of those bustle skirts that were so popular in the 1880s. Amanda's a very slim, petite woman, but this lad took one look at her and shouted, "Blimey, she's got a big bum, ain't she?" '

MAKE-UP

The finishing touches came from Sue Milton, who's provided hair and make-up for TV series as diverse as *Moll Flanders*, *In a Land of Plenty* and *Cracker*. Like her colleagues in the wardrobe department, Milton was responsible not only for the lead characters but also for the crowd scenes.

'We've had some very busy days on location,' she says. 'When we've got the whole family in, and they're at some social function, we're getting people in at the crack of dawn to get them ready. Some of the character make-up takes up to an hour and a quarter, but then you've got to make sure that everyone else who appears on camera looks convincingly in period. The biggest problem I've faced on *The Forsyte Saga* is that young men just don't have hair any more. They all have a number-one or a number-two crop, so there's nothing you can do with that except stick a wig on it. We've used a lot of wigs on this show! It's funny: ten or twenty years ago, when lads had longer hair, they were all really reluctant to get it cut if we were doing something that was set, say, in the twenties. Now they've got no hair at all. The ballroom scenes are the hardest: you have to find supporting artists who can dance, and who fit the costumes, and then I'm left at the end of the line going, "But he's got no hair!" '

Fortunately for Sue Milton and her team, most of the leading actors not only have their own hair, but are at the right age to play convincingly below and above their years. An actor like Damian Lewis, who was thirty during the filming of *The Forsyte Saga*, would find that any misguided David Beckham-inspired haircuts might substantially reduce his casting opportunities. 'Damian's got beautiful red hair,' says Milton, 'which we really had to plaster down to his head to make it look less lively, and to give him that severity that Soames would have aimed for. It's not just oiled: it's absolutely stuck down tight onto his skull. All the men dressed their hair to some extent, but not that severely. Bosinney's hair, in contrast, is freer and floppier. It's not quite Oscar Wilde length, but it's getting there; it's certainly long enough to have caused comment among the Forsytes.' Milton added a few discreet extra locks at the front of Ioan Gruffudd's hair to emphasise his unconventional, romantic look.

The rest of the cast can be pinpointed accurately within the social spectrum according

A maternity dress for Hélène.

to the way they wear their hair. 'People always tend to find a style that suits them, and it usually comes from the period when they were fairly young and at their most attractive. Our first scene is set in the mid-1870s, and some of the older ladies have hairdos that hark right back to the 1820s, when they would have been fashionable young girls just starting out on life. If you look through photographs and paintings from the period, you'll see that people tended to go for one look and stick to it. Queen Victoria, for instance, had quite curly hair when she was younger, but then she adopted that very severe, pulled-down look and she wore her hair that way until she died.

Amanda Root looking jaunty at a fitting for Winifred's costumes. While (right) Ioan Gruffudd looks suitably dashing and romantic in his loose-fitting coat.

I've seen pictures of men who were young at the time of Waterloo, who sported whiskers and haircuts that stayed exactly the same for the next sixty years – they just got greyer! People were like living museum pieces. I suppose the same is true today: once you get past your experimental stage, and you enter into middle life, you don't change your appearance that much. You can tell a lot about a character like Montague Dartie from the way he wears his hair. He's quite a stylish creature, because he's interested in impressing people – not just the Forsyte family, but also the girls he meets at the theatres. So he has rather smart, well-cut hair and a very stylised moustache, curled and nicely

dressed. He's very different from Soames, who is completely clean-shaven.'

Thus we'll see the older generation – particularly Aunt Hester and Aunt Juley – sporting the styles of the 1830s, already way out of fashion by the time the story starts. 'Juley [Wendy Craig] comes across as quite a silly, girly character, so I've given her those sausage curls at the side of the face that bob around when she moves. I'm sure she looked enchanting as a young maid.'

The younger women change more throughout the story as they move into maturity. 'Irene starts out quite girlish: she has a fringe in the first episode, which makes Gina look very young. Once she's a married woman, the hair goes up and becomes more formal, more severe – although I've left Irene's hair fairly loose because she's not as conventional as the rest of the family. Her hair is also a reflection of her social position. She starts off in relative poverty, and she has to do her own hair. But, once she marries Soames, she has a lot more money around her and she can afford a maid to come and take care of things. So the hair becomes more stylised, more elaborate – she's moved up a class. When she falls from grace and leaves Soames, her hair becomes softer again. It expresses her freedom, and also her lack of money.'

(above left) The dressers ensure that even the extras' costumes are absolutely perfect.

(above right) A busy day on set: a team of make-up artists work on a continual stream of actors.

Damian's hair had to be plastered to his head to make it look less lively and give him the severity needed for Soames.

(Above right) The men's hair – or rather lack of it – caused the most problems. (below left and right) Putting the finishing touches to the ballroom hair.

Make-up was used principally to indicate the ageing process – women in the period would have worn very little apart from a touch of rouge in the cheeks or on the lips (only ladies of the night, or actresses, wore full slap). 'We have to make everyone look as young as possible in the early episodes, then gradually age them up. What Sita [Williams, the producer] did not want was any obvious ageing make-up, so everything was done very subtly. You can suggest age by a certain pallor of the skin, or by prosthetic eye bags, but you certainly won't see any lines drawn on people's faces. There's a little bit of shading round the eyes – again, that can age someone up – but that's about as far as it goes. Soames stays very similar throughout, even though he's ageing over twenty years; you'll just see a little bit of grey coming into his hair. With some actors, I've covered up the grey in the earlier episodes and then let it show later on; others are natural to start with then have a bit of grey added.'

Overall, the look is neither strikingly 'period' nor jarringly modern. It's fitting for a writer like Galsworthy, who occupies a transitional place in English literature, that any adaptation of his work should look to the present as well as to the past. 'I didn't want to labour the fact that this is a costume drama, a period piece,' says the producer, Sita

Williams, 'because that brings so much negative baggage with it. On the other hand, I'm not one of these producers who try to fight shy of the fact that they're representing life as it was a hundred years ago. There's no point in saying, "This is a really contemporary piece, they're just like us!" because that's not true: manners and morals and behaviour and dress were very different at the turn of the century. This was before the First World War, before women had the vote, when a lot of the freedoms that we take for granted now were only dreamt of by a few social radicals. It's daft to have people running around like twenty-first-century characters in a nineteenth-century story. What I hope we've achieved is something that has the richness and strangeness of a time gone by, but which also makes a very direct appeal to a contemporary audience through the eternal things it says about human nature.'

THE ACTORS' STORIES

'Soames is such an ambiguous role. I don't expect the audience to like him, but I want them to understand him.'

DAMIAN LEWIS

Damian Lewis was, as he puts it, 'whoring myself' in Los Angeles at the beginning of 2000, looking for film work after completing Steven Spielberg and Tom Hanks's *Band of Brothers*, when he got a call from the producers of *The Forsyte Saga*. 'From that point

on it all happened very quickly. We had a meeting, they asked me if I wanted to be Soames and I said yes. Then I had the enviable job of sitting there with strings of gorgeous and talented actresses reading with me for the part of Irene.'

It's a good indication of the kind of status that Lewis, now 31, has reached in recent years. In the mid-nineties, after appearing in *Hamlet* on Broadway, he made his first exploratory visit to Hollywood, decided the time wasn't right, came back and made *Warriors* (Peter Kosminsky's award-winning drama about peacekeepers in Bosnia) and *Hearts and Bones*, then landed the role in *Band of Brothers*. 'Now I don't really have to audition for jobs. I just have these very grown-up meetings. It's not that everyone's suddenly offering me jobs outright – it's just that I now tend to be one of three or four that they're considering, rather than one of two hundred and fifty who's up for the job.'

The character of Soames appealed because, says Lewis, 'it's such an ambiguous role. I don't expect the audience to like him, but I want them to understand him. He's not sympathetic, he's emotionally repressed and supercilious, he has a smug, condescending way of dealing with people. But you also see him genuinely distressed and in pain, driven to the desperate act of raping his wife. It's the act by which he's judged, and the series will only become interesting if the audience struggles between hating him for it and sympathising with what's driven him to it. If they simply detest him, it will be a lot less interesting.'

Now that *Band of Brothers* has gone out to universal acclaim, and with *The Forsyte Saga* set to consolidate his position with British audiences, Lewis finds himself in a very different position from this time last year. 'I don't know what to expect. I'm hoping that the phone will start ringing a lot more, because there was a huge buzz about both of the shows. Until we've got some reaction to *The Forsyte Saga*, I've no idea what kind of direction I'll go in. I'm in a state of flux, really. I just sold my house: I'd been living with my brother for the last three years, and he got married so we decided to get rid of the house. So although I live in London, I don't actually have a place there at the moment, apart from my girlfriend's and a room in a friend's house where I keep a lot of stuff. When we were filming *The Forsyte Saga*, I had a flat on Canal Street in Manchester, which was pretty lively. I'm rather enjoying the experience of being homeless, and I'm in no hurry to buy a place. It's nice to have the loose change, having just sold a house. I can do really responsible things like buying sports cars.'

GINA McKEE

Released for the afternoon from the corsets and bustles of the 1880s, Gina McKee is trying to get comfortable in her trailer on the Liverpool location for *The Forsyte Saga*. 'Look at me! I usually have good posture, but I'm slouching deliberately. I think it's a way of getting back at all those awful uptight Forsytes!'

There's no ambiguity in McKee's attitude to her character: Irene's a victim of her time, of her circumstances and most particularly of the Forsyte family. 'She's a woman of spirit and intelligence, and there's no way she was ever going to fit in with that lot. I don't know if anyone could ever truly fit in with that sort of family — she says bitterly! They repress her and stifle her, and then as soon as she starts to emerge as an independent woman they turn on her. Her spirit is badly damaged by what happens to her, although I'm glad to say that she gets it together eventually.'

McKee's reluctant to talk about the key scenes in the disintegration of Soames and

Irene's marriage, 'because I don't want to give anything undue prominence, when it's all really part of the process. If you discuss the rape, then it becomes "that rape scene", and people forget everything else. Suffice to say that we've shot it, it's not just a sexual act, it's about power and possession and even punishment to a certain extent. And it wasn't rape, of course: you couldn't rape within marriage. It's a very curious situation for a woman to be in.'

There's more to Irene than victimhood, though, and McKee is keen to portray her as a self-determined character. 'It's quite hard to do that while honouring the spirit of the times, because a spirited woman in the Victorian period would have been very repressed and restrained. She's constantly beaten down by this idea of duty, which becomes her prison, but she struggles against it in her own rather passive way. She doesn't actively revolt: she just freezes Soames out. She's too honest to pretend to love him; she won't play the game. But, when real love comes

'I'm happy to say that, in her passive way, Irene persecutes Soames as much as Soames persecutes her.'

along, it takes her by storm. She doesn't know what to do. The feeling consumes her, but it doesn't make her happy.

'There's a wonderful scene at the ball when she finally admits to Bosinney, without actually saying the words, that she loves him. That admission means that her life is in free fall. She'll have no income, no position, no support; she'll be to all intents and purposes a fallen woman. All the Forsytes immediately assume that she turns to prostitution. A divorce was the worst thing that could happen to a woman, but Irene's intelligent enough to realise that it brings a tremendous liberation as well. She doesn't care any more – they can't hurt her. She becomes the most tremendous thorn in the family's side, and I'm happy to say that, in her passive way, she persecutes Soames just as much as he persecutes her.'

RUPERT GRAVES

'Young Jolyon is the antithesis of Soames.'

As Forsytes go, Young Jolyon is one of the most relaxed and forward looking; compared to Soames, he's a social radical. 'I see him as a pioneer of the arts and crafts movement,' says Rupert Graves. 'He suffers from the Forsyte curse of not being able to express his emotions and be a mature human being in that respect, but he does pretty well compared to most of them. He is, at least, conscious of that aspect of his character, and he tries to do something about it. He's propelled by his feelings of love and beauty, rather than by self-interest or respectability. I keep thinking about Prince Charles: he's a man from a very uptight background who seems to be struggling with it, whose impulse is towards freedom and honesty but who can't quite make the break.'

'Bosinney's a rebel, basically: he stirs people up, and that's always an attractive part to play.'

Jolyon is the nearest thing *The Forsyte Saga* has to a romantic hero, and it's fair to say that audiences will respond warmly to the relationship that grows in later episodes between him and Irene. 'That was the highlight of the series for me,' says Graves. 'You see their first meeting, and there's clearly some kind of spark of sympathy between them, but neither of them is in a position to do anything about it. Then, when Jolyon's wife is dead and Irene has lost Bosinney, they manage to work towards each other. All the stuff that's set in Paris is very good, even if most of it was shot in the Wirral, which is a pretty poor substitute for the real thing.'

Young Jolyon's function in *The Forsyte Saga* seems, largely, to be as a foil to the central struggles of Soames. The two men are polar opposites, and have a cordial dislike of each other from the very first page. It's tempting to see Jolyon as a Galsworthy self-portrait – particularly as Irene seems to represent Ada, the woman he wrested from an unhappy marriage with his own cousin. 'Jolyon is the antithesis of Soames,' says Graves. 'While Soames stays in town and observes all the rules, Jolyon runs away and lives an almost hippy lifestyle, with a vegetable patch, no money and no staff working for him. Faced with an unhappy marriage, as he is at the beginning of the story, he'd rather make a clean break, whereas Soames tries to keep up appearances and ends up making his wife hate him. Jolyon is hot-headed and says things he regrets; Soames is cold and calculating. Every time you see us on screen together, the contrast becomes more and more obvious.'

Jolyon, of course, has the luxury of being a rebel with a very rich family to fall back on. 'He comes back into the fold and starts living at Robin Hill, which is very nice for all concerned. I think it's the reward Galsworthy gives him for being a decent human being. He's one of the few characters who actually learns lessons from life and grows up in the course of the story, so I'd say that he deserves it.'

IOAN GRUFFUDD

'I had reservations about doing another period drama,' says Ioan Gruffudd, who's most closely associated with roles such as Hornblower and Pip in the BBC adaptation of *Great Expectations*. 'But that all changed as soon as I read the scripts, and particularly when I screen-tested with Gina McKee. She's just about my favourite actress. I've seen all her work and I just think she has such taste and class. I guess you could say that influenced my decision.'

Bosinney may seem, at first glance, to be the unalloyed romantic hero of *The Forsyte Saga*, but, like all the characters, he's an unclassifiable mixture of good and bad qualities.

'I think he comes across as rather pompous, to be honest,' says Gruffudd. 'He's incredibly confident, and he has total belief in what he's doing as an architect. He's ahead of his time, and he's impatient with people who aren't up to speed with him. That wrong-foots people, makes them wary of him. He's a rebel, basically; he stirs people up, and that's always an attractive part to play. But his behaviour towards June is pretty unforgivable, even though you realise that he's fallen head over heels in love with Irene. He's quite selfish, and he's capable of trampling over other people to get what he wants. I suppose he gets away with a lot because he's charming.'

'I'm sure that Galsworthy identified strongly with his female characters and I'd like to think that there's a lot of him in Winifred.'

This is the first time that Gruffudd has worked with Damian Lewis since their memorable performances in *Warriors*. 'This is a complete reversal of our roles in that film. In *Warriors* I was the staid, in-control one, and Damian was more flashy. This time it's the other way round.' It's also Gruffudd's first job since he finished shooting *102 Dalmatians* at the end of 2000. 'I did nothing at all for the first half of 2001. It wasn't planned that way: I was just out of the way doing *102 Dalmatians* for six months and I wasn't around to go for jobs. So when *The Forsyte Saga* came along I was itching to get back to work. And of course Bosinney is out of the show by Episode Three, so it wasn't a terribly long commitment. That's always attractive to an actor.'

AMANDA ROOT

'Winifred is the only one of the Forsytes who understands what makes the family tick, who can be simultaneously part of it and yet maintain a bit of critical distance,' says Amanda Root. 'That's the beauty of her character. She pushes the envelope a bit. That's why she marries Dartie: he's a loose cannon, he's roguish, and he shakes things up for the family. I think there's a mischievous streak in Winifred, which makes her more fun to play.'

Ever since she starred in the BBC's adaptation of Jane Austen's *Persuasion* in 1995, Root's been very much at home in nineteenth-century costume. 'It's given me a great deal of insight into how much we've gained as women in the last hundred years. Women were basically enslaved in the Victorian period. The clothes were a physical manifestation of their social position. Wearing corsets and stays, it's actually very hard to breathe. You can't walk without assistance, you can't work, it's hard to eat and you're prone to fainting. No wonder it was such a threat to men when women started rejecting these clothes: suddenly they were able to walk and work and run and do all the things that a man could do.'

Winifred Galsworthy is often read as proof of Galsworthy's sympathy with the emergent feminist movement. There's no doubt that he believed in the emancipation of women, says Root. 'The interesting thing about *The Forsyte Saga* is that it covers a transitional period, when new attitudes were emerging, and the novels form a fantastic document of that change. Winifred embodies a lot of that. She's much more modern than her brother; she's the sort of girl who will just say to hell with the etiquette, let's dance and have a good time and not care what anybody thinks about us. On the other hand, she's still sufficiently part of the Forsyte clan to want to avoid scandal and to keep up appearances. If she'd been part of the younger generation, she'd have been much more rebellious. As it is, she takes big strides forward. I'm sure that Galsworthy identified strongly with his female characters, and I like to think that there's a lot of him in Winifred.'

BEN MILES

'I do feel as if I'm on *Stars in their Eyes* sometimes,' says Ben Miles, who plays the ne'er-do-well Montague Dartie. 'It's the moustache. One day I'm going to look into the camera and say "Tonight, Matthew, I'm going to be Freddie Mercury." ' Dartie is a dapper fellow, and Miles certainly gets the best of the men's wardrobe in *The Forsyte Saga*. 'He tries to be overly English, because he's from a slightly lower social level than the Forsytes so he's trying to compensate. There's one school of thought that says he's from a Jewish background, which would make sense – he's trying to curry favour with a class not known for its sympathetic attitude towards Jews. The English upper classes were terribly anti-Semitic at this time. It works with the Forsytes because, let's face it, they're not the cleverest family in the world.'

Miles is used to playing attractive smoothies, most recently in BBC2's hit comedy *Coupling*, and he sees the key to Dartie's survival in the family in his ability to charm

Winifred. 'There's a very strong bond between them, and, even though he's an absolute sod to her and runs off to Buenos Aires, she takes him back. She loves him because he's a bit of a rough diamond, he's got style and wit, and we must assume that they have a great sex life. He loves her because she's intelligent and funny as well as rich. He desperately craves her approval and forgiveness, but he acts like a child as soon as he's reproved. They have big slanging matches. He's one of the few characters who ever loses his temper and gets a bit carried away. He's the polar opposite to Soames: he's the Technicolor to Soames's black and white.'

GILLIAN KEARNEY

As soon as she was cast in the role of June Forsyte, Gillian Kearney got cracking with some research. 'I looked at a lot of paintings and photographs of women in the period, and I took deportment lessons to try to get the moves right. There were a lot of strict rules about how you would address people, how much you would touch each other in public, which influence the performance a good deal. Mind you, you have to play the situation as if it's really happening to you, so you can't go around the whole time as if you're balancing two books on your head.'

'We must assume that they [Winifred and Dartie] have a great sex life.'

This is Kearney's first major costume role; since she left *Brookside* (where she played Damon Grant's love interest, Debbie, and went on to star in the short-lived spin-off *Damon and Debbie*) she's appeared in Debbie Horsfield's *Sex and Chips and Rock 'n' Roll* and the school drama, *Hope and Glory*, with Lenny Henry. 'Actors love doing period

'Actors love doing period stuff because it's a chance to be really proper. It's like real, grown-up acting.'

stuff because it's a chance to be really proper. It's like real, grown-up acting. But for me the attraction is that June changes a lot over six episodes. I start off as a 17-year-old girl who's madly in love and quite naïve, and by the end of the series I'm quite a worldly woman who understands the way the family works. She learns from her experiences and she's not afraid to tell people what she thinks. There's a terrific scene between me and Gina [McKee, as Irene] where I tell her that she's ruined my life, and she ends up slapping me around the face. Most of the time the characters are so restrained that a scene like that is shocking by contrast.'

THE
FORSYTE
SAGA

HOW DO YOU TURN TWO SIZEABLE NOVELS
INTO SIX EPISODES OF DRAMATIC
TELEVISION? HERE'S HOW: AN
EPISODE-BY-EPISODE GUIDE TO THE FORSYTE
SAGA AS IT UNFOLDS ON THE SCREEN.
BE WARNED: PLOT LINES ARE REVEALED!

EPISODE ONE

To all appearance, the Forsyte family are a united clan – united by ties of marriage, money and a social code that values respectability above all else. But all that's about to be blown apart. While the family gathers in James and Emily's home in Park Lane to meet Winifred's new fiancé Montague Dartie, Young Jolyon is at home fretting over the ill health of his little daughter, June. It soon becomes apparent from looks and words exchanged over the child's sickbed that Young Jolyon is in love – not with his wife, Frances, but with the child's governess, Helene. To the Forsytes, this kind of behaviour is absolutely unthinkable – it breaks the rules of class, of marriage, of property. Nothing is said at this point, but much is understood.

Winifred introduces her fiancé to the assembled Forsytes.

Meanwhile, at the family gathering, Dartie is trying hard to impress his future in-laws. He and Winifred are clearly in love, and enjoy laughing at the family behind their back – but it's also clear that Dartie is desperate to get his hands on some of the Forsyte loot. The elderly aunts are impressed by this handsome newcomer, but Soames isn't so sure.

The romantic tension between Young Jolyon and Helene is growing. Frances confronts her husband, who assures her that nothing has 'happened' – but Frances, realising that Helene is a clear and present danger to her marriage, insists that the governess be dismissed. Young Jolyon is forced to confront his feelings, and in an attempt to give Helene the sack he ends up kissing her. An ugly showdown with Frances ensues; she realises that her attempts to salvage her marriage have actually forced her husband into the arms of another. This is not the only time this will happen in *The Forsyte Saga*. Young

Jolyon decides to follow his heart, even if it means losing his beloved daughter June. He announces the decision to his father, who is forced by the family code to disown his son. A painful scene ensues, in which Old Jolyon tells Young Jolyon that from this point on he will assume that his son is dead.

Four years have passed. Under pressure from his family to marry and provide an heir to the Forsyte property, Soames is on the lookout for a wife. A business trip to Bournemouth throws him into the path of Mrs Heron, a widower who's struggling to bring up her stepdaughter, Irene, on a very limited income. Soames is immediately struck by Irene's beauty, and starts to accompany mother and daughter to concerts and exhibitions, finding endless excuses to pop down to Bournemouth 'on business'. And, for Soames and Mrs Heron, this *is* business: he's keen to get an heir, and she's eager to get this expensive stepdaughter off her hands, with a comfortable settlement on herself, she hopes. While suitor and mother hammer out the terms of the arrangement, Irene finds herself completely out of sympathy with Soames. He is stiff and formal, she is warm and spontaneous; they could hardly be worse suited. Mrs Heron, however, twists Irene's

One of Young Jolyon's many sketches of Hélène.

In deep mourning. Irene and Mrs Heron after the funeral.

(Above and right) Soames travelled up and down to Bournemouth in order to pursue Irene, despite the fact that she showed no interest in marrying him.

arm, pointing out that she's hardly in a position to be choosy and that offers like Soames's don't come along every day. For now, Irene insists on waiting for something better to present itself – but she's too much of a realist to think that she can afford to wait for ever.

Young Jolyon, now officially the black sheep of the family, has settled down with Helene and their illegitimate son, Jolly. They are broke, and so Young Jolyon is obliged to go cap in hand to his uncle James to ask for some of the money that was left to him by his grandfather. James refuses to release the money on moral grounds; he's a trustee of his father's will, and uses this power to punish Young

Jolyon for his defection from the Forsyte clan. Soames thoroughly approves of his father's decision – and, of course, it was Soames who made sure that his father reached the 'right' decision.

Soames is keeping up the pressure on Irene, escorting her round London, impressing her with his wealth and social standing. Irene insists that she cannot be 'bought', but agrees to meet the family – it seems she doesn't really have much choice. At a ball in Park Lane, Irene dazzles with her beauty, and shocks the family by dancing – strictly speaking she's still in mourning for her father, and should be sitting down and keeping quiet. Winifred is absolutely delighted to meet a kindred spirit, and relishes the chance to shake up the stuffed-shirt Forsytes. Soames, intoxicated by the sight of Irene dancing, manages to take her for a few turns around the floor, and falls desperately in love with her. Or is it just lust? For the first time, we realise that there's more to Soames than meets the eye.

He becomes more than ever determined to catch Irene, and follows her home to Bournemouth, where he proposes repeatedly to her. She can't stand him – but a violent row with her

June and Bosinney in happier times.

stepmother persuades her that she'd better take any offer that's going. She negotiates an agreement with Soames whereby he will 'release' her if the marriage does not work out. Soames, convinced that love will come (and in truth only concerned about possessing Irene and making her have a son), gives his word. It's hardly a romantic arrangement, but Soames has got what he wants – or so he thinks.

Time passes, and Young Jolyon's abandoned daughter June has grown up into a young

woman, raised by her grandfather. Her mother has died, she knows nothing of her father, now remarried with two children of his own. June is a new sort of woman in the Forsyte family – intelligent, independent, with a mind of her own. She tells Old Jolyon that she's met a young man whom she wants to marry – his name's Philip Bosinney, he's an architect, he's penniless at the moment but bound to be rich soon. Old Jolyon grudgingly agrees to an engagement, but insists that Bosinney must have at least £400 a year before they marry. He can't deny June anything – she's the light of his life.

Married life isn't working out too well for Soames and Irene. They've moved into a beautiful house in Montpelier Square, she has more money than she's ever dreamed of – but there is no love. When Soames kisses her, she recoils – and, after they've had sex, she douches to make sure she doesn't get pregnant. The rest of the family are keen to know why there are no children on the way, little guessing that Irene can barely stand to see Soames, let alone bear his child. Shrinking from all physical contact, she insists that she should have her own room. Soames is horrified: what will the servants think?

June, meanwhile, is head-over-heels in love with young Phil Bosinney, whom she introduces to the family as her husband-to-be. She even brings him to church, where the gossip is flying about Soames's marriage. Is it true that they have separate rooms? And why hasn't she had children? Bosinney, intrigued by talk of this mysterious woman, catches Irene's eye across the church. And they hold each other's gaze for just a little too long …

After repeatedly refusing him, Irene finally accepts Soames's proposal following a violent row with her stepmother.

EPISODE TWO

Aunt Ann, the oldest surviving Forsyte, has died at the age of 86, leaving Old Jolyon the head of the family. The surviving Forsytes gather at the Bower on Bayswater Road, home of the aunts, to mourn Ann's passing and to pass on the family gossip. Bosinney is there with June, feeling very much the outsider, but happy to have another chance to meet Irene. They are awkward and formal together – particularly as Soames is ever-present, like a watchful hawk. As yet, however, he has no suspicions about Bosinney, and enlists his support in a plan to build a new house out of town, a place where he and Irene can live far from the stresses and strains of town. Irene is to be kept in the dark; this is to be Soames's surprise for her. Bosinney, conscious that a commission from Soames would give him enough money to marry June, eagerly accepts the proposal.

Aunt Ann's coffin lying in state at the Bower House.

Fired with enthusiasm, Bosinney and Soames travel down to Robin Hill, the spot near Richmond that Soames has bought for his new house. Bosinney, with his artist's eye, is enraptured by the place: the views are beautiful, and he will build Soames a house worthy of the location. Soames at first is full of practical concerns but eventually, seduced by Bosinney's passion, he agrees to a really spectacular commission. Perhaps, he thinks, a beautiful house in the country will make Irene love him – and it will remove her from the bad influences of London.

Bosinney tells June of his success – now, of course, they can marry. June is delighted, and doesn't notice that Bosinney seems just a little less enthusiastic about the forthcoming wedding than he should be. At a chance meeting with Irene in Hyde Park, June tells her that Soames is building her a lovely new house in the country. Irene turns away, choked with horror at the prospect of this new prison – and Bosinney's heart is torn by the sight of this beautiful woman trapped in a loveless marriage. Headstrong June, however, is oblivious of the undercurrents, and sees no reason why Irene shouldn't be happy for them and happy to have a new home.

Old Jolyon, conscious that time is running out for him, is missing his son terribly. It's many years since they parted on bitter terms, and Old Jolyon has never even met his two grandchildren. Swallowing the Forsyte family pride, he seeks out Young Jolyon at his club, and after an awkward few moments father and son are reconciled. Young Jolyon takes his father home to meet the family. At first there's tension between Helene

After many years
of estrangement
Old Jolyon meets
his son's second
family.

and her father-in-law: has he just come to get his hands on his grandchildren? Isn't it a bit late for reconciliations? But Young Jolyon reveals that his father has been secretly supporting them all these years by buying Young Jolyon's paintings. It's time to let the past go, to forgive and forget.

Things aren't going so well for Winifred. Her marriage to Montague Dartie has been blessed with two children, Val and Imogen, but Dartie's turned out to be a bad egg and is forever getting into trouble with his gambling debts. Winifred's been turning a blind eye, handing out money and keeping mum to the rest of the family, but one day the bailiffs turn up at their house in Green Street and seize the furniture. James turns up just in time to witness his daughter's disgrace, and there's a furious scene.

Soames's marriage is faring even worse. He's furious that the family are gossiping about the sleeping arrangements in Montpelier Square, and confronts Irene with a *fait accompli*: they will go and live in the country, far from London, and they will have children. Irene recoils from the idea – for her the marriage was over a long time ago, and she remembers Soames's promise to set her free if things didn't work out. And now, to add to her problems, she's falling in love with Bosinney, her best friend's fiancé. Bosinney visits Montpelier Square to go over the plans for Robin Hill with Soames,

but it's really Irene he's come to visit – and, in a quiet moment undisturbed by Soames, they kiss for the first time. For Irene, there's no turning back; at last she knows what love is really like. If only she'd met Bosinney all those years ago! Soames is blind to what's going on right under his nose, but June isn't so blind. She senses Bosinney's neglect of her, and is quick to divine the reason.

As Soames's marriage falls apart, his house at Robin Hill is coming along nicely. Bosinney is doing a wonderful job, but it's expensive – and Soames is watching every penny. Architect and client find themselves arguing furiously at every turn – and it's apparent that they're not just fighting over money. Soames is beginning to realise that this man represents a threat to his property, but typically he's careful not to fall into open dispute with Bosinney, whatever the causes. He wouldn't want to jeopardise the

Winifred's marriage to Dartie is a troubled affair as she copes with his roving eye and gambling debts.

Bosinney and Irene confess their feelings for each other.

95

building plans, after all, or for people to ask why they fell out. Instead, he invites Bosinney and June to dine with him and Irene. This is not a good idea under the circumstances. June can see quite plainly what Soames chooses to ignore, and storms out of the dinner when the sexual tension between Irene and Bosinney becomes too much for her. She pleads with Bosinney to let her be 'nice' to him in his rooms, but he's miles away, and June realises that she's lost him.

Looking stiff and uneasy at a family gathering, Irene and Soames find it impossible to communicate.

Irene finds an excuse to pop down to Robin Hill to inspect the building works – suddenly, it's of interest to her. She 'accidentally' meets Bosinney there, and they manage to snatch a few moments of privacy in the woods. The spring flowers are blooming all around them, the air is fresh and clean, the sun is shining, and inevitably they fall into each other's arms.

The Forsyte gossip machine springs into action. Why is June looking so sad? Is it true what they're saying about Irene and Bosinney? Dartie takes advantage of Irene's slightly tarnished reputation by groping her at a family get-together, witnessed by Bosinney. A huge row ensues, during which Bosinney announces that he's not going to marry June; he then sweeps Irene onto the dance floor, oblivious of the family's censorious gaze. Soames's frustration is pitiful to behold, and he confronts Irene with his suspicions. Far from bringing her to heel, this pushes Irene out on a limb, and she asks Soames for the freedom that he promised her long ago, before their marriage. And out in the street, thinking himself unobserved, Bosinney gazes up at the house that contains the woman he loves.

EPISODE THREE

Three days after the fatal ball at which Irene and Bosinney stepped beyond the point of no return, Soames continues to pretend that nothing's wrong and even proposes that he might take Irene on a nice holiday, away from all their troubles. But it's no good: she's

Falling deeper in love: following the ball, Bosinney and Irene grow ever closer.

growing more and more distant, and is clearly just going through the motions of living with Soames to avoid a scandal. Soames is boiling up with anger and frustration, and on a visit to view the completed building at Robin Hill he picks a fight with Bosinney over money. The bill's £350 more than they'd agreed – and Soames, pretending that he's just protecting the principles of good business, threatens Bosinney with legal action for breach of contract. Nobody, not even Soames's adoring parents, are fooled by this, but the threat soon becomes a reality and the legal wheels start turning.

Old and Young
Jolyon, together
again.

There's nothing the Forsytes love more than a good legal case. They're lawyers, after all, and it gives them something to get their teeth into – while giving the aunts something to gossip about. Irene and Bosinney, thrown closer together by Soames's open hostility, are meeting secretly at his chambers, trying to enjoy their affair but constantly harried by the threat of ruin. Bosinney's optimistic, until word gets out that he's in dispute with Soames – and he finds that the ranks of society are closing against him. Nobody will commission new work from him, he's fast becoming *persona non grata*, and he realises

Hélène and Holly: despite their poverty Hélène and Young Jolyon were very happy.

that Soames is bent on destroying him as punishment for his wife's desertion.

June returns from a therapeutic holiday on the continent with Old Jolyon, during which she's done her best to forget about Bosinney and turn over a new leaf. Arriving in London, she's horrified to hear about the impending court case, realising at once that it will only serve to throw Irene and Bosinney closer together – and this she does not want to see. Try as she might, she can't switch off her feelings for Bosinney, and it pierces her to the quick to see him falling ever deeper in love with Irene. The affair is fast becoming public knowledge, as people speculate as to the real cause of Soames's fight with Bosinney – and, try as they might, the lovers can't keep the affair secret for long. Young Jolyon sees them together in the Park, and at last Irene realises that she has taken the decisive step towards separation, and all the disgrace that will ensue.

Montpelier Square where Soames has his town house.

Old Jolyon, disgusted by Soames's vindictive behaviour, withdraws his legal business from the family firm and makes an independent settlement on Young Jolyon and Helene, with whom he has now effected a full reconciliation. He offers to buy them a house, convinced that their bohemian existence in St John's Wood is not entirely comfortable for them. Helene at first is too proud to accept, but Young Jolyon convinces her that it's for the best, and that he would happily leave the family all over again if it only meant he could hold on to her.

As one conflict resolves itself, another is coming to a crisis. Life in Montpelier Square is becoming intolerable, as Soames begins to insist on his conjugal rights. One night, after drinking too much, he comes uninvited into Irene's room and forces her to have sex with him – it's his right as a husband, he insists, and she has no choice in the matter. The following morning, Soames tries to pretend that nothing untoward has happened, but Irene flees to Bosinney and bursts into tears, confessing what Soames has done to her. Bosinney storms off to find Soames and extract his revenge for wrecking his life and raping the woman he loves. He bursts into the office, causes a scene at Soames's club and is thrown out onto the street – and then, blind with rage, Bosinney falls under the wheels of a carriage.

Unaware of the accident, Soames proceeds with his legal action against Bosinney.

There are awkward scenes in the courtroom when Bosinney fails to turn up for the hearing; Soames assumes he's just run away, but June is not so sure and goes looking for him. Irene, meanwhile, is waiting for her lover in a hotel in Waterloo, her bags packed – they have arranged to leave the country as soon as the case is heard. But Bosinney does not come, and Irene, frantic with worry, rushes to his rooms to see what has happened. There she meets June, and the two women – still ignorant of Bosinney's fate – argue bitterly over the man they both love. It's the end of a once fine friendship, and they part after Irene has slapped June's face. Irene is left alone with nowhere to go, apparently deserted by her lover.

Irene's disappearance throws the Forsytes into a panic. This is what they feared most – not the misery of an unhappy marriage, not the violence or the harsh words or the conjugal rape, but an open scandal. Soames and his father go in search of Irene, desperate to avoid the shame of a separation – and then the police arrive to request Soames's assistance at the mortuary. A body has been found with no identification other than some court papers that name Mr Forsyte; it is, of course, Bosinney. Soames returns home in a daze; all he can think of is that Irene will now return to him because her lover is dead.

Irene, meanwhile, is wandering around London searching for Bosinney. In desperation she gains entrance to the men-only Hotch Potch Club, where Young Jolyon finds her and breaks the news of Bosinney's death. It's too much for Irene, who collapses in shock. Young Jolyon, much against his judgment, takes her back to Montpelier Square – back to her husband. And, as he leaves her there to face an uncertain future, Young Jolyon sees the bruises on Irene's arm, evidence of Soames's recent assault. Has he made a terrible mistake?

Countdown to tragedy: the carriage that seals Bosinney's fate.

EPISODE FOUR

Despite her shock over Bosinney's death, Irene dare not stay in Montpelier Square and so, in the small hours of the morning after her return, she takes off her wedding ring and leaves for ever. Soames has to confront the fact that she's not coming back, that he has driven her away – but, as usual, his prime concern seems to be with minimising the scandal and making sure that the servants don't gossip. He races down to Bournemouth, imagining that Irene would have returned to her stepmother, but of course she is not there.

Old Jolyon falls in love with Irene.

June is also grieving for Bosinney, and under these awkward circumstances she meets her father, Young Jolyon, for the first time since he too deserted the family home. It's a painful moment, but both father and daughter want to put the past behind them and move on. Besides, June's too preoccupied with her own troubles to ponder too long on her father's past – she's got a bone to pick with Soames, whom she blames squarely for Bosinney's death. At the funeral, she confronts Soames with the truth about his marriage, about Irene's hatred of him, about why they never had children. Soames keeps a stiff upper lip, but June's words have hurt him very deeply. Everything he did was for Irene, or so he believes. He adored her, and he wanted nothing more than for her to love him in return and have his children. Was that so wrong? At a kind word from his sister Winifred, Soames lets down his guard for once in his life and cries over Irene's departure. He takes to his bed and allows himself to be 'ill' for a few days. Emily attempts to comfort him, but it's impossible for mother and son to show real, spontaneous affection for each other, and they end up speaking bitterly of Soames's childhood. Soames decides that the only medicine is to pretend that nothing's wrong, and he goes back to work.

For all his coldness, Soames grieves deeply at Irene's departure.

Old Jolyon has been as good as his word and has bought a house for his son and grandchildren – and not just any old house, either. He's bought Robin Hill. Soames is never going to live there, that much is clear, and it's standing empty now that Bosinney's dead. And so, as the younger generation take possession, Robin Hill at last becomes what it was always meant to be: a family home, full of children and laughter and love.

Five years have passed with no contact between Soames and Irene. Helene has died, Young Jolyon has gone on holiday to Spain with June, and Old Jolyon is holding the fort at Robin Hill with only his granddaughter, Holly, for company. And then one day, walking the dog in the grounds, he sees a familiar figure sitting on a log looking out at the view. It's Irene. She has come to see the house that Bosinney built, the house that could have been her home. Old Jolyon, somewhat shy in the presence of this beautiful young woman, shows her over the property and finds out a little about how she's living. She's alone, there has been no one since Bosinney, and she makes her money by giving music lessons to children. A friendship blossoms between the old man and the young woman, both of them lonely, both of them tied to Robin Hill by memory and affection. Irene visits often on the pretext of teaching little Holly the piano, but it's really to see Old Jolyon. Both realise how much

Old Jolyon, much-
loved and much-
missed at his
death.

Father and
daughter: June and
Young Jolyon
comfort each other
following Old
Jolyon's funeral.

the family would disapprove of this strange friendship, and when June comes home
from her holiday they are forced to part.

Needless to say, this new liaison has not gone unnoticed by the Forsyte spies – Old
Jolyon has been seen at the opera with Irene, and riding in the Park. Everyone is quick
to jump to conclusions: Irene must be after Old Jolyon's money, and must of course have
hopped into bed with him. Soames is the first to believe and condemn, conveniently
omitting to mention the fact that he's been making weekly visits to a prostitute who just
happens to look a lot like Irene.

Old Jolyon dies, and his will reveals that he's left a substantial amount of money to
Irene. The clan gather for the funeral at Robin Hill, eager to pick over the bones of this
latest piece of gossip. Young Jolyon – who is still a black sheep as far as most of the
family are concerned, despite his reconciliation with his father – delivers a very pointed
eulogy of his father, describing him as 'a giant among pygmies'. The criticism does not
go unnoticed, and Soames stalks off in a bad humour. Amid all this love, he is alone with
his conscience.

June is bereft at the loss of her grandfather; he, after all, is the one who brought her
up, and then as soon as her back was turned he fell in love with Irene. Just like
Bosinney! But Young Jolyon assures her that she, June, was the one person whom Old
Jolyon really loved. Young Jolyon himself, however, is less certain of his own feelings for
Irene. They meet to discuss the terms of Old Jolyon's will, and each realises that there
is a sympathy between them that might have come to something under different
circumstances. But, for Irene, the time has come to distance herself from the whole
brood of Forsytes.

EPISODE FIVE

It's 1899, seven years after the death of Old Jolyon, and Soames is celebrating his 45th birthday at a big family gathering. Not that he's got much to celebrate – his hopes that Irene might one day return to him have been dashed, and he's lived in a depressing limbo ever since the day she left Montpelier Square. There's some light on the horizon: he's met a nice young French girl, Annette, the first woman he's really been attracted to since Irene, and he'd like to marry her. But there's an obstacle: he's still married to Irene, having refused to seek a divorce at the time of Bosinney's death. His squeamishness about scandal all those years ago has trapped him in a position from which he can see no escape; after all, there's no evidence that Irene has been unfaithful, and the only alternative would be for Soames himself to commit adultery, which of course would be unthinkable. And so he pursues a pointless courtship of Annette, and continues with his perfunctory weekly visits to a prostitute.

For once, though, Soames's feelings get the better of him, and he invites Annette and her mother to see his new house at Mapledurham. They are impressed: here is a man who could offer Annette a really comfortable future, a far cry from her current situation as the daughter of a Soho restaurateuse. It's a struggle for Soames to express his

A desperate man: Soames persuades Young Jolyon to make contact with Irene.

affection for Annette, and he's embarrassed by her class, but the courtship goes ahead nevertheless.

Winifred's marriage has gone from bad to worse. Dartie, it turns out, isn't only a lecher but a thief as well – he's taken a string of pearls from Winifred's bedroom to give to one of his girlfriends. And not just any old pearls, either – these are the jewels that he gave Winifred on the occasion of Imogen's birth. Winifred confronts him over the theft, and Dartie causes an enormous scene, claiming that he's hard done by, and waving a revolver around, threatening suicide. It's all bravado, but Dartie's tongue gets the better of him: he insults Winifred, admits he gave the pearls

Upholding the family feud: Val and Jolly fight over Holly.

Against the odds: Holly and Val fall in love

Dartie dips in his wife's jewellery box.

to a younger woman and tells her that their marriage is over. Winifred can stand no more, and Dartie, realising that he's burned his bridges, sneaks out of the house. Soames is on the case the following morning, advising his sister to seek a divorce as quickly and quietly as possible, not to put herself into the no-man's-land that he currently inhabits, 'married yet unmarried'. Winifred is swayed by his advice, but cannot understand why he's suddenly so keen on divorce. Would it have anything to do, perchance, with Irene?

Soames pushes Winifred's divorce case relentlessly onwards, and realises that he too must seek to resolve his own marital situation. Knowing that Young Jolyon is the trustee of his father's will, Soames asks for news of Irene – and Jolyon admits that he has some limited contact with her, in the form of an annual letter in return for the allowance cheque. Soames persuades Jolyon to make contact with Irene and to ask, on his behalf, if she will provide him with grounds for a divorce. Jolyon, who can't stand his cousin, agrees to ask Irene if she is seeing anyone – but he will not press Soames's case with her any further than that. Soames grudgingly agrees to these terms.

Jolyon carries out his promise, and goes to visit Irene in her Chelsea flat. She is still young, still beautiful – and still single. There are no grounds for divorce. This is not what Soames wants to hear, and so he pays a call on his wife in person, intending to be masterful but quickly melting in her presence. The old desire, the old obsession, has not abated, and before he knows it Soames is begging Irene to come back to him and give him a son. He's wasting his breath, and Irene struggles from his grasp. Terrified of another visit, Irene decides to leave London and live obscurely in Paris. Young Jolyon, hearing the news, curses Soames for driving her away.

Soames decides that he must get a divorce at all costs – as long as it involves him in no personal scandal. And so he sets about an absurd 'investigation' of Irene, hiring a firm of private detectives to find her and to provide evidence of adultery. They track Irene to Paris, and find her in the company of Young Jolyon, who has followed her there on the flimsiest of pretexts. Soames, hearing the news, is stung by jealousy; he still loves Irene in his fashion, and cannot bear the idea of losing her to his hated cousin.

When he confesses his feelings to Winifred, he's astonished at her furious response: he forced her to go through a divorce hearing and now he tells her that he wants to take Irene back? And so, when Dartie returns home with his tail between his legs, fresh from a disastrous sojourn in Buenos Aires, Winifred defiantly takes him back. The divorce is off.

Irene and Young Jolyon grow ever-closer.

The dissent in the Forsyte ranks is already beginning to make itself felt in the younger generation. Val Dartie, Winifred's son, has met and fallen in love with Holly Forsyte, Jolyon's daughter by Helene. This comes swiftly to the attention of Jolly, Holly's priggish brother, who fights with Val and ends up making a stupid wager that they will both enlist in the army to go and fight in the Boer War. Val tells his family that he's going to war – but he doesn't reveal the real reason. The older generation are thrilled at such a patriotic action, but Winifred and Jolyon are both frightened and dismayed.

The warm friendship between Irene and Young Jolyon is fast growing into love, fuelled by Soames's continued persecution of his wife. As Jolyon rushes home to see his son off to war, he and Irene kiss for the first time – under the eyes of the ever-present private detective.

EPISODE SIX

As the rest of the family prepare to do their bit for the Boer War, Winifred is adjusting to the unexpected return of her errant husband. Dartie would like to forget that anything ever happened, and within days he's sponging off Winifred, lusting after other women and generally playing the cad. Winifred goes for comfort to her mother, but such is the restraint between the two women that they can't hug or cry in each other's presence, and Emily is reduced to expressing her maternal concern through boiled eggs and cups of tea. It's not easy for Dartie, either: he quickly realises that his own son is ashamed of him, and he's terrified that his beloved daughter Imogen will find out what Daddy was really up to in Buenos Aires. Dartie and Winifred agree to let bygones be bygones, but nobody would expect theirs to be a happy ending.

The time has come when Val and Jolly must leave for South Africa, and the family gather at the army barracks to see them off. It's a typical Forsyte family affair: nobody can say what they really mean, and everyone's eager to find out as much family gossip as possible. Imogen is intrigued to see the Jolyon branch of the family for the first time,

Val in his uniform, preparing to leave for South Africa.

and demands to know why she's never been introduced to her cousins before. As the older generation cough and blush to cover their embarrassment, Val and Holly sneak off to say their private farewells. And Young Jolyon, realising that he might never see his son again, breaks with family tradition and actually hugs the boy.

Poor old Soames is still pursuing Irene, oblivious of the fact that he's become a figure of fun in his own office. Nobody, not even the private detectives, are convinced by his charade that he's just gathering information for a divorce – but Soames, as usual, thinks he's playing a very clever game. Discovering that his wife is living in Paris, he tracks her down to the Bois de Boulogne and makes one final, desperate attempt to bring her home. He'll do anything: they can live separately, he won't pester her, he just wants her to give him a child. They argue in public – witnessed, of course, by the self-same private detective whom Soames has hired to spy on Irene. Later he's seen coming out of her hotel room, where he's gone to leave a note, but Irene is one step ahead of him and has already fled.

On returning home, Soames has a meeting with the head of the detective agency, who announces a triumphant piece of news: the party in question has finally been seen in a compromising position with a man in a Paris park, and the same man was seen

The Dartie family: Imogen, Winifred and Montague bid farewell to Val.

Soames and Annette. Soames never felt the same passion for Annette as he had for Irene.

coming out of her hotel room. His description? 'Pale red hair, guilty look and manner ...' Soames, recognising the absurdity of his situation, dismisses the laughing detective from his offices. Days later, however, news comes that Irene has been seen again, much closer to home. She's been visiting Young Jolyon at Robin Hill. This, at last, is the 'proof' that vindictive Soames has been waiting for, and he springs into action.

The affection of Paris has now turned into love at Robin Hill. Irene comforted Jolyon after the news that his son, Jolly, had been killed in the Boer War, and now they are beginning to realise that they could make some kind of future together. And, at the crucial moment, enter Soames, ranting and raving about adultery, threatening to horsewhip Jolyon. He couldn't push the two lovers together more successfully if he tried, and Irene stands up to him and defies him to do his worst. Yes, she says, we are lovers; go ahead and get your divorce; we won't stand in your way; we have nothing to lose.

Soames finally gives up and starts behaving like a rational human being. He has lost Irene, but he still has a great deal to offer the right woman: a secure income, a beautiful home at Mapledurham, children and a family. Fortunately for him, Annette is still willing to listen to his suit, and a deal is struck that suits all parties. Not the most romantic of marriages, perhaps, but Soames has had enough of romance. He packs up all of Irene's dresses and jewellery and, after one last despairing erotic frenzy, finally lets her go.

Val returns from the Boer War with an injured leg and a surprise for his mother: he's married Holly Forsyte, and they're going to start a new life in South Africa. Soames, too, is making a new start: he's married Annette, and they're expecting a child. And, in a trio of happy endings, Young Jolyon marries Irene, who gives him a son, Jon. The final reconciliation comes when June arrives at Irene's bedside to offer the olive branch. The bitterness of Bosinney's death is all forgotten and forgiven. It's the end of an era: Queen

Victoria is dead, and the family gather in Park Lane to watch her funeral procession go past their windows.

Our last sight of Jolly as he marches to war.

For Soames, though, there is one more great drama. Annette goes into labour, but there are complications. The doctor announces that he can save either the mother, or the baby – but in the former case Anette will never be able to have another child. Soames is obsessed by the desire to produce an heir: his father is dying, and the family must be continued. He tells the doctor not to operate, to risk Annette's life for the sake of the baby's. To his relief, mother and baby both survive. Soames can barely stifle his disappointment when Annette tells him that he's got a daughter. And, at James's deathbed, Soames tells his father that he has – a son. James dies in peace.

Soames returns home, bitter and dejected after the death of his father. He can hardly face Annette – he would have let her die, and now he's disappointed in the birth of his daughter, who must be his only child. Against all his Forsyte instincts, he bends over the cot and looks into the face of the child, his daughter, Fleur – and, as he gazes down at the baby, his heart softens.

WHO'S WHO

SOAMES FORSYTE

Born in 1855, Soames is in his early twenties when the story starts, but to all intents and purposes he's a middle-aged man already. Soames is the embodiment of the Forsyte spirit – industrious, proper, hard-working, resourceful and completely out of touch with his own emotions. It's a fact recognised by Aunt Ann, the head of the family,

who adores her uptight nephew and recognises that he's the one who ought to be carrying on the family name and producing another generation of little Forsytes.

And there's nothing Soames would like more than to be a Victorian paterfamilias, with a fragrant wife and a brood of children, among them a son who's just like him. But things don't work out that way, and unfortunately for Soames he falls passionately in love with Irene. Being Soames, of course, he doesn't recognise the nature of this love. So while he's burning with sexual passion on the inside, tormented by jealousy and desire, he keeps a stiff upper lip and pretends that theirs is a polite, conventional courtship and that she will be a polite, conventional wife. He must have known better from the start, but Soames's intuitions are buried so deeply beneath his starched shirt front that he can't or won't take notice of them. And so, for the rest of the story, Soames is on the rack, trying to force messy reality into the acceptable patterns of Forsytism – sometimes with tragic results. His inhuman treatment of Irene, his chilly hostility towards his family, his own self-consuming rages, are all the result of frustrated passion.

When Soames builds Robin Hill as a dream home-cum-gilded cage for Irene, the family dub him 'the Man of Property' – and it's a truer nickname than they might have guessed. Everything, to Soames, is a possession. His house is an investment, it's never a home. He collects art, not because he loves it but because it might gain in value. A wife, too, is just another piece of property that will make him look good in the eyes of society, and will give him a son to carry on the family business. It's significant that the only time we see Soames having consensual sex with a woman, she's a prostitute – a woman that he has bought for the hour. He never even knows her name.

Yet, for all this, Soames is a sympathetic, even a lovable figure. Galsworthy may have set out hating him – and there's evidence to suggest that *The Man of Property* was based on his own cousin Arthur, the first husband of his wife, Ada. But, by the time he started to write *The Forsyte Saga*, Galsworthy began to see that there was a heart underneath that starched shirt, and that Soames embodied all the contradictions and ambiguities of his class. Halfway through the story, we begin to understand what makes him tick; by the time he's stuck in the limbo of his failed marriage, we might almost like him. He will always turn round and do something incredibly stupid and inappropriate, pushing away even the people who love him the most; but, for all that, Soames can't be rejected altogether, even at his worst. It's greatly to Galsworthy's credit that he created a character with so many flaws – a greedy materialist, cynical and sneering, a man capable of raping his own wife – in whom we could still feel an affectionate interest.

In the later novels, Soames becomes a venerable old codger, content in his marriage to Annette, more and more like his bewildered father, James. He can only express his deeper emotions to children and animals – and there's the biggest clue of all that Galsworthy, that 'stuffed shirt' with his love of dogs, recognised in Soames some essential part of himself.

IRENE FORSYTE, NÉE HERON

The Irene whom we see on screen is by necessity a different person from the Irene of the novels. In Galsworthy's prose, Irene is a nebulous figure, a force of nature rather than a person in her own right. She is defined almost entirely by the effect she has on other people, particularly men, who are instantly drawn to her incredible sexual attractiveness. Soames wants her to be the ideal Victorian wife – a hostess, a mother, and, presumably, a red-hot lover behind closed doors. Bosinney sees her as a romantic heroine, a sort of pre-Raphaelite vision trapped in the high tower of her marriage, a

damsel whom he must rescue from the wicked Bluebeard Soames. To Old Jolyon, she represents youth, freedom and vitality, a 'second chance' at life. And to Young Jolyon – the only man who sees her as a human being first, and a woman second – she is an ideal companion. But, then, Young Jolyon has had enough women in his time not to be dazzled by Irene's looks.

Irene is a woman just ahead of her time. With a little education and opportunity, she could have been happily independent, perhaps even a campaigner for women's rights. But hers is the sad reality of many Victorian women, denied financial independence, obliged to be dependent on husbands for any kind of respectable life. She lacks the courage to break out on her own – Irene may be a victim, but she's responsible to some extent for her own problems. When we first meet her, she's in mourning for her recently dead father, and facing life with a stepmother whom she cordially dislikes. Then, realising that her prospects are pretty grim, she agrees to a marriage with Soames, naïvely believing that if it doesn't work out she will be 'free'. Of course it doesn't work out, and Irene, like a sulky child, refuses even to try to make a go of it. She wants love, and nothing but, and when she finds that Soames is never going to be her knight in shining armour she takes back her toys and refuses to play any more. The contrast with Soames's second wife, the pragmatic, unromantic Annette, could hardly be greater.

Apart from her tendency to sulk, Irene is an almost flawless personality. She is honest – a little too honest at times – and would never stoop to using her looks for gain. The life she dreams of with Bosinney is a bohemian idyll, love in a hut – she cares nothing for money, or so she says. And, after Bosinney's death, she keeps clear of men and concentrates instead on helping fallen women, recognising that she could so easily have become one herself. Indeed, Irene is always lucky: a chance meeting with Old Jolyon leads to a substantial inheritance, which saves her from the painful business of earning a living. She is brave under persecution from Soames, flirtatious and almost fun when she meets Young Jolyon, and capable of turning heads right through to the very end.

Like Soames, Irene is neither all bad nor all good. If this was really a portrait of Galsworthy's wife, Ada, let us hope that she was sufficiently flattered to overlook some of Irene's less appealing characteristics.

PHILIP BOSINNEY

Young Phil Bosinney is the answer to a young girl's dreams. Dashingly handsome, talented and unconventional, he appeals to the rebel in women like June and Irene, and he outrages the more conservative elements of the Forsyte clan. This is a chap, after all, who would wear a soft hat to a funeral – shocking! The fact is that he can't afford the more acceptable topper, which of course makes him only more attractive to impulsive young women with a fortune at their disposal. Cynical observers dub him 'the Buccaneer', assuming that he's using his looks and charm to hook himself a rich wife in much the

same way as Dartie did – and, while there may be a grain of truth in this, it's more likely that Bosinney just allows such plums to fall in his lap without having to shake the tree too much.

At a time when most of the professional classes are indistinguishable in their conformity, Bosinney is a tearaway. His ideas about architecture are way ahead of their time; he believes in a creed of love and beauty, which he expresses through his work and his personal appearance. His hair is just a little too long, his shirts a shade too colourful – he teeters on the edge of aestheticism. This was a time, after all, when Oscar Wilde was sauntering down Piccadilly with a lily in his hand, and Bosinney would not have felt out of place in such rarefied circles.

Bosinney is the anti-Soames. He's everything that his rival isn't: warm, spontaneous, impetuous, passionate. He doesn't give a damn what people think of him, and he has a cavalier attitude towards money. The world owes him a living, and he would rather concentrate on immediate pleasures than worry about the future. It's an incredibly seductive attitude, and even

Soames finds himself being sucked into Bosinney's world-view to some extent. To women it's irresistible. But Bosinney isn't altogether admirable. His treatment of June is disappointingly shabby – he doesn't have the courage to tell her their relationship is over, preferring to pass by her in the street without saying a word. He's heedless of women's reputations, and leads Irene into danger without adequate circumspection. He's untrustworthy, too: when Irene's meant to be running away with him, she can't banish the suspicion that he's let her down. Bosinney, the romantic hero of *The Forsyte Saga*, is an idol with feet of clay.

WINIFRED DARTIE, NÉE FORSYTE

There's a rogue gene somewhere in the Forsyte line, and it comes out in full force in Winifred, Soames's younger sister. Winifred is a clever woman: bright enough to laugh at the rest of her family, but sensible enough to stay within the fold and to roll with the punches. She enjoys the privileges of her class too much to do without them, but all the same she has a satirical spirit, and is ready to stand up against her bullying brother when he tries to push her too far. Compared with uptight Soames and gloomy Irene, Winifred is a breath of fresh air.

Her great weakness, of course, is her husband, Montague Dar tie. Dartie is a bit of a cad, and a woman of Winifred's intelligence would have seen that right from the start. She marries him nonetheless, partly because he's handsome and sexy and jolly good fun, but partly, we suspect, to cock a snook at her family and to introduce a bit of a spark into the bloodline. She puts up with Monty's extravagances and infidelities with stoic good humour – she knew what she was letting herself in for, after all. But when Monty goes too far, openly insults Winifred and tries to steal from her, she has to retreat behind the shield of Forsyte family honour. She's a tough person, but not that tough.

Unlike her brother, though, Winifred understands the meaning of forgiveness. She would rather make a compromise than stand up for some ridiculous principle. This doesn't make for a wholly happy family life, but at least she keeps her marriage going. She shocks Soames by refusing to get a divorce, but the results speak for themselves.

Winifred is in many ways a transitional figure, with one foot in the Forsyte camp, the other stepping towards the future. She has sufficient intelligence to question the sexist assumptions of her class, but that's about as far as it goes. There's a telling scene when, at the height of her marital problems, she goes to her mother for comfort. Neither Winifred nor Emily is capable of reaching out and touching the other, and both have to express their sorrow and concern through the stilted, formal language of contemporary manners. But, compared with her brother, Winifred is a barrel of laughs.

MONTAGUE DARTIE

Son of a once wealthy family who lost all their money, Montague Dartie has good looks and an easy charm – formidable weapons in the search for a wealthy wife. How his eyes must have lit up when he got Winifred Forsyte in his sights: here's a woman of means, not unattractive, who's on the lookout for a bit of a rough diamond just such as himself. Dartie is man-of-the-world enough to know that posh girls like a bit of rough, and so he's

quite rude with his 'Freddie' while maintaining the sleek outer surface required by the rest of the family. The strategy works well, and Dartie marries into money.

Sadly for all, the Forsytes aren't quite as easily won over as Winifred. Dartie was hoping for a great big marriage settlement that he could then have squandered on the gee-gees, but instead he finds that they're on an allowance and living in a rented house in Green Street – not at all what he'd envisaged. From that point on, married life is never quite what it might have been for Monty and Freddie. They have two lovely children, Imogen and Val, but Dartie's an absent father, busy chasing dancers and borrowing money. For all his swagger and charm, Dartie's a coward and a bully, and when Winifred catches him stealing her pearls to give to a dancer he resorts to cruelty, then runs away from his responsibilities.

Dartie's adventures in Buenos Aires are comically murky; all we know is that he comes back to Winifred with his tail between his legs, and spends the rest of

the story as a bit of a joke, desperate to retain the respect of his daughter, the only one in the family who doesn't see straight through him. But, for all his failings, Dartie's not stupid. He recognises the more venal side of human nature – he should, he's an expert – and can see what's going on underneath the polite surface of a Forsyte family party. He recognises the attraction between Bosinney and Irene (but of course, being Monty, he thinks this means he can have a go at Irene himself). He's quick to discern Soames's failings, and can always cut through the cant to the baser motive beneath. This doesn't make him particularly likable, but he's a necessary foil to his repressed in-laws. And Winifred never stops loving him, for all his faults.

OLD JOLYON FORSYTE

In a family of fuddy-duddies, Jolyon Forsyte Sr stands out like a beacon of decency and sanity – a giant among pygmies, as his son describes him. He's one of the most thoroughly likable characters in the entire Forsyte saga, and this could be because he was drawn from life, a portrait of Galsworthy's beloved father. Jolyon represents the Forsyte spirit in its most benign aspect: he's a pioneer, an accumulator of wealth, resourceful and brave, quick to anger but equally ready to forgive. Unlike his brother James's side of the family, Jolyon can always see two sides to an argument. He has a quick, hot temper that makes him say and do things he regrets, but he's prepared to listen to his heart and make up for his actions. He possesses the very un-Forsyte-like quality of knowing when he's wrong, and actually admitting it.

We first meet Old Jolyon as a typical Victorian patriarch, throwing his son out when he discovers he's having an affair with the governess, swearing that he'll never see him again, writing him out of his will. But, as the story proceeds, Old Jolyon melts. He misses his son, he's saddened by the knowledge that he has two grandchildren whom he's never met, and he realises that Young Jolyon may have done the right thing by leaving a woman he never loved. And so, to make up for his mistake, Old Jolyon secretly supports his son by buying his paintings – and, of course, raises his daughter June without a murmur. In time he realises that this love-at-a-distance isn't enough, and he rebuilds bridges that were burned long ago. The *rapprochement* between father and son and the growing relationship with the grandchildren comprise one of the most touching sequences in all the Forsyte stories.

Old Jolyon is not just a nice twinkly old granddad: he's a man capable of strong emotion, as he discovers, somewhat to his surprise, when he befriends Irene. The love that grows between them is, perforce, platonic, although we are well aware the Old Jolyon would like it to be otherwise. His defiance of family censure, and his defence of Irene, is the moral highpoint of his life; and his death – at peace in the gardens of Robin Hill, with the people he loves at hand – is an example of Galsworthy at his very best.

YOUNG JOLYON FORSYTE

Despite their differences, Jolyon Jr is very much his father's son. He's guided by his heart rather than his head – and, when he finds that he's fallen in love with his daughter's governess, he's quick to act. Not for him the long, drawn-out agony of a typical Forsyte marriage, soldiering on despite the fact that the two parties can't stand the sight of each other. Jolyon realises at once that he has to cut and run, for his own good and the good of his wife, Frances (at least, that's the way he sees it; she might think otherwise). He renounces the twin gods of Forsytism, money and respectability, and runs away with Helene to live a life of scandalous poverty, having children out of wedlock and eking out an existence in a series of grotty flats. The fact that he can be happy under these circumstances is a terrible insult to the rest of the family, who would much rather he came crawling back or at least had the   decency to die.

As he grows older, Jolyon makes his peace with the family and with society at large. He's not a hothead, doesn't see any essential virtue in poverty, and, when his father makes him the very generous offer of Robin Hill, he's happy to accept. Money is the making of Jolyon, because it means he can afford to be generous. He's a wonderful father to Holly and Jolly, and even manages to patch things up with June, the daughter he abandoned when she was a child. Like Bosinney, Jolyon is an artist, and that seems to make him irresistible to women. It's tempting to see elements of self-portraiture in his character; perhaps this is how Galsworthy liked to see himself, as a romantic outsider.

Jolyon and Soames can never get on – they're like chalk and cheese. Their fathers, James and Old Jolyon, have never been good friends, and the differences are simply

magnified in the sons. It's inevitable, then, that, when Young Jolyon befriends Irene, Soames will immediately be on the defensive. It's his persecution of the lovers that drives them into each other's arms – typically, Soames manages to achieve the very end he was trying to prevent. And in Irene Jolyon finds lasting happiness. They also produce a son, Jon, who will continue to plague Soames in the later novels.

JUNE FORSYTE

By rights, June should have had an easy life. Beautiful and intelligent, she's born into a good family and has comfortable financial expectations. But June's just one of those people for whom things never go right. First of all, her father runs off with the governess, after they've shared an intimate moment over baby June's sick bed. Then the man she loves runs off with her best friend. Then her beloved grandfather falls for the same woman and promptly drops dead. Then, to cap it all, her own father, with whom she's reunited after a lifetime's separation, goes and marries the same woman again. Little wonder that June is wary of men!

With all this misfortune raining down on her, June Forsyte should be a bitter old maid, but luckily for her she's inherited her father's ability to adapt to circumstances, and remains plucky and cheerful throughout. Well, most of the time, anyway: she's capable of tremendous rages, and says some wickedly cruel things to Soames and Irene, but at least she gets it out of her system and moves on with her life, unlike the others, who tend to sit in corners, brooding.

If June has a fault, it's her recklessness. She meddles in Irene's marriage, spilling the beans about Robin Hill, and pays the price by losing Bosinney. She is forever picking fights with Soames, shooting her mouth off and making things worse for everyone. But June learns from her mistakes, and comes back from her time on the Continent a more mature and considerate person. In the later novels, she takes up a role as the slightly eccentric spinster, dabbling in art and keeping a spiky distance from the rest of the family – for which you can hardly blame her.

JAMES FORSYTE

Soames and Winifred's father is a gloomy old stick. He's never had an original thought in his life, and if he did he'd have kept it to himself. He's terrified by the idea that life is somehow slipping out of his control – and indeed it is. It's James's misfortune to live in an era of rapid, frightening change, when the certainties of the Empire he grew up in are being supplanted, when even religion is being questioned. He cannot understand why the younger generation doesn't just get on with things and stop complaining; it's incomprehensible to James that a woman like Irene should walk out of a respectable marriage, for instance.

James's great obsession is with continuing the family line. He tells Soames at every opportunity that he must have a son; even on his deathbed he's possessed by the idea. This does nobody any good. It cranks up the pressure on Soames, who wants nothing more in life than to please his father; and it hurts Winifred, who of course has already provided a son in the shape of Val, only to have him largely overlooked by his grandfather. James isn't particularly bright in this respect: it would never occur to him that he was damaging his children. He's not terribly bright in business, either: it's Soames who has all the ideas and keeps the firm going. James is content to see his investments growing, and turns a blind eye to everything else. It's this blindness that keeps him in the dark. James is forever complaining that nobody ever tells him anything, but considering his amazing resistance to facts this is hardly surprising.

EMILY FORSYTE, NÉE GOLDING

Emily is a good wife. She may not be a very happy one, but she's certainly a good one. She's put up with James not because she particularly loves him, but because it's her duty. She's raised two children along the strict lines of Victorian parenting, and does not really wish to know when they have problems or worries in adult life. Her response to Soames's emotional traumas over Irene is to say that she should have beaten him more in infancy.

Like most of the Forsyte women, Emily is more intelligent and intuitive than the men. She can see what's happening under her nose, and she may even wish to do something about it, but she would never have the guts to step out of line. Unlike the aunts, who see only what they want to see, Emily understands that life can't always be put into neat little boxes. She's learned from her

marriage to James that the myth of the ideal family is based on hard work, self-denial and eternal compromise. This she sees as nothing more than her duty. In a later generation, Emily might have stood up for herself a bit more, but as it is she's willing to sacrifice everything on the altar of the Family.

THE AUNTS: ANN, JULEY, HESTER

In Galsworthy's novels, there are ten children in the Forsyte family – which makes the first few chapters of *The Man of Property* extremely difficult to follow. These have been culled somewhat for television purposes, leaving us with three elderly aunts and the rather shadowy figure of Uncle Swithin, whose purpose in life seems to be to get the wrong end of the stick and to nod off when he's not wanted.

The remaining aunts are a comical crew. Ancient Aunt Ann is a formidable spinster about whom we know little apart from the fact that she has an almost fanatical devotion to her favourite nephew, Soames. Her sisters, Julia ('Juley') and Hester, are almost stock characters of English literature, gossipy old ladies who make up for the dullness of their own lives by taking a voracious

interest in the doings of others. Juley was married once, to one Septimus Small, who died of a weak constitution and left her with a rather blurred memory of married life. The more severe Hester never managed to get herself a husband, and so had more time to devote to observing the peccadilloes of others. After the death of Ann, the two ladies lead an increasingly pointless life in the Bower on Bayswater Road, popping out for weddings and funerals, fortunate only in the Forsyte family wealth, which will never leave them wanting.

THE YOUNG ONES:
VAL, IMOGEN, JOLLY AND HOLLY

The Forsyte family tree has developed so far along two main branches, headed up by James and Jolyon. There is very little communication between the two: Soames loathes his cousin, Young Jolyon, and everything that happens in the story serves to push the families further apart. Winifred's children, Val and

Imogen, have inherited some of their father's happy-go-lucky attitude, while Jolyon's offspring, Jolly and Holly, are used to a bohemian lifestyle where the normal rules don't really apply. Thus it's not that surprising that, when the junior members meet up, there should be curiosity and a good deal of attraction.

Val Dartie meets Holly Forsyte. They have some smashing romps on horseback out at Robin Hill, and rather predictably fall in love. Jolly turns out to be something of a prig who disapproves of the match; he would really have been more at home as a son of Soames, whom he resembles more than he does his father. Circumstances conspire to wipe Jolly out of the story, leaving Val and Holly to start a new life together in South Africa. Imogen, who's been kept in the dark as all nice young ladies should be, never really understands what all the trouble was about in the first place.

Above: Val Dartie; Bottom far left: Holly Forsyte, Below left: Jolly Forsyte; Below right: Imogen Dartie

CAST LIST
(IN ALPHABETICAL ORDER)

ANNETTE	BEATRICE BATARDA
AUNT ANN	JUDY CAMPBELL
AUNT HESTER	ANN BALL
AUNT JULEY	WENDY CRAIG
BOSINNEY	IOAN GRUFFUDD
EMILY FORSYTE	BARBARA FLYNN
GEORGE	ALISTAIR PETRIE
HÉLÈNE HILMER	AMANDA OOMS
HOLLY	AMANDA RYAN
IMOGEN	ALICE PATTERN
IRENE FORSYTE	GINA MCKEE
JAMES FORSYTE	JOHN CARLISLE
JOLLY (AGED 7)	JACK LANGHAM
JOLLY	CHRISTIAN COULSON
JUNE (AGED 14)	JESSICA FOX
JUNE	GILLIAN KEARNEY
MADAME LAMOTTE	KIKA MARKHAM
MONTAGUE DARTIE	BEN MILES
MRS HERON	JOANNA DAVID
OLD JOLYON	CORIN REDGRAVE
SOAMES FORSYTE	DAMIAN LEWIS
SWITHIN	ROBERT LANG
VAL	JULIAN OVENDEN
WINIFRED	AMANDA ROOT
YOUNG JOLYON	RUPERT GRAVES

PRODUCTION CREDITS

PRODUCER	SITA WILLIAMS	
DIRECTOR	CHRISTOPHER MENAUL	1 – 3
DIRECTOR	DAVID MOORE	4 – 6
WRITER	JAN MCVERRY	3, 4, 5
WRITER	STEPHEN MALLATRATT	1, 2, 6
SCRIPT EXECUTIVE	ROXY SPENCER	
DESIGNER	STEPHEN FINEREN	
DOP	SUE GIBSON BSC	1 – 3
DOP	ALAN ALMOND BSC	4 – 6
COMPOSER	GEOFFREY BURGON	
COSTUME DESIGNER	PHOEBE DE GAYE	
MAKE-UP DESIGNER	SUE MILTON	
CASTING DIRECTOR	JUDI HAYFIELD	
SCRIPT EDITOR	JULIE PRESS	
SCRIPT SUPERVISOR	HILDA MILLER	
EDITOR	TONY CRANSTOUN	1 – 3
EDITOR	ANTHONY HAM GBFE	4 – 6
SOUND RECORDIST	PHIL SMITH	
ASSOCIATE DESIGNER	DESMOND CROWE	
ART DIRECTOR	NICK WILKINSON	1 – 3
ART DIRECTOR	PETER BULL	1 – 3
1ST ASSISTANT DIRECTOR	SAM HARRIS	1 – 3
1ST ASSISTANT DIRECTOR	VINCENT FAHY	4 – 6
UNIT PUBLICIST	JANICE TROUP	
LINE PRODUCER	THEA HARVEY	
HEAD OF PRODUCTION	SUSY LIDDELL	
EXECUTIVE PRODUCER	ANDY HARRIES	